Visualizing Ideas  From Scribbles To Storyboards

Thames & Hudson

Thinking like a pro...

We're creative and thoughtful – and we really know how to get things done.

We're pragmatic. Layouts are not an end in themselves: they just help us to sell ideas.

We're honest. Layouts with no ideas behind them are worthless. Showiness is not the same as style.

We're professionals, and we do only what we have to do to get our ideas across. No more, no less.

We like the work we produce. That means that we can always argue in support of all of our presentations.

We're inquisitive. Until we've got an idea that's good enough, we never stop looking for better alternatives.

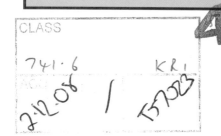

We have ideas. And when we don't have an idea, we don't stop till we find a good one.

3

We're flexible. Good ideas can be put down on paper any time and anywhere.

We know what's most important – getting our clients to believe in our good ideas, so that they won't buy bad ideas from anyone else.

We're fast. That saves time, money and energy.

Contents: themes & techniques

4

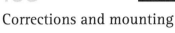

5

Anyone can design a layout...

...but only a few people know it. Whether you use stick figures or fully rendered illustrations or photographs, a few rough lines or a detailed diagram, there are many different ways to make an idea visual. For an illustrated proposal to get its message across, the designer must make sure that the signs, codes and visual short cuts that are chosen can be understood by the target audience.

As authors of this book, we don't want to promote a particular style of visualization (although of course we have our own trademark styles). What we want to do instead is to motivate people to express themselves visually – simply, quickly and in a way that can be easily understood. Our layout tips are the result of many years' work for agencies and as freelancers, and of experience gained as lecturers at a technical college geared towards practical work. Most of the work shown here was created by students at the Design Faculty of the University of Applied Sciences in Wiesbaden, Germany, and it goes to show that anyone can develop a personalized layout style within a very short space of time.

From head to hand to paper. In the beginning, original ideas for ads, posters or films only exist in the minds of designers, eventually moving from there onto paper. It doesn't matter whether it is a drawing pad or the edge of a paper tablecloth, at an agency office or between the starter and the main course at a restaurant. This book aims to encourage artistic spontaneity, quick doodles and effectively drawn layouts. You'll learn that the right stroke of a pen – or a mouse – can be your ticket to freedom and independence – and can be great fun too.

Visualize your ideas quickly, simply and punchily. Fresh new graphic ideas come from thought, imagination and intuition – and the mind they come from could be yours. These are the hallmarks of a creator, the true author of a design. Flicking through magazines, design yearbooks and other printed sources unfortunately only encourages you to make dull copies of ideas that have already used. Computers are also often abused in order to give a stylish sheen to uninspired ideas, rather than being seen as the purpose-orientated, hi-tech tools they actually are. Plagiarism is commonplace: it's a sign of the wilful exploitation of someone else's creativity and at the same time an indication of your own deficiencies.

Once you've got a starting point, the image has to leave your mind so that it can be presented and convince a third party – the client, in other words – of its quality. A layout turns an idea into something concrete, gives it substance and allows important decisions to be made. You are, of course, free to use any style, media or form of presentation. However, despite all the technical possibilities of photocopying and scanning written material, it is graphic visualization – strangely enough – that offers the most variety with the least effort.

The biggest advantage of a graphic approach is the freedom to come up with any image from memory, anywhere and at any time. And no technical equipment is required. A pen and paper can always be found, so it's hardly surprising that many a legendary campaign allegedly originated on the edge of a paper tablecloth or a napkin in a bar or restaurant.

Layouts are just a means to an end. But you need to know where you're going. Professional layouts are unambiguous and leave no room for misunderstanding. A layout is basically a visual aid: it allows you to argue and convince. It acts as an introduction to an overall idea, and lets you look ahead towards later stages of development. A layout is a useful tool for selling ideas and not an end in itself. Once the presentation at the client's offices is over, the task of the layout is more or less complete. It then becomes simply an aid to implementation: a guide for the ad director or photographer, for example.

Thumbnails and sketches are your first steps. But there's always the chance you might stumble. There are different kinds of layout, depending on who is going to see the design and why. The approach taken should be varied according to the needs of the agency and the client, as the various examples in this book show.

Nesrin Schlempp-Ülker is a designer and freelance illustrator who teaches layout design at the University of Applied Sciences, Wiesbaden.

Gregor Krisztian has spent many years as an art director in advertising agencies and works as a communications designer and writer. Since 1984 he has been a professor in the Design Department of the University of Applied Sciences, Wiesbaden.

As a rule, in the beginning comes a rough doodle or thumbnail. Often small in scale, it uses a few strokes to sketch out a visual idea or sequence, rough positioning of text and compositional variations. Thumbnails are seldom suitable for presenting to clients. Yet there are exceptions, even here, especially when the clients know their creative partners and trust in their abilities. However, thumbnails are generally only used for internal discussion and decision-making.

Thumbnails therefore need to show the idea that lies behind them. The next step is the rough layout, which explores the basic idea in more detail. Here we usually work at full-size format, allowing us to tell if the composition or colour scheme accurately reflects the initial idea. The art director, copywriter and everyone else who has a say at the agency can now get a good idea of the formal strengths and weaknesses of the project to be tackled and carry out any necessary changes and improvements.

Moodboards are another form of visual shorthand, designed to express the atmospheric qualities and moods of the target group. In themselves they do not depict a concrete idea, but instead try to get across the emotional content of a particular lifestyle or environment.

Professional layouts skip unnecessary details. Once the final composition and art direction have been agreed on, the layout is frequently reworked to produce a comprehensive layout. This is then presented to the client. It is not unusual for layout artists and illustrators to come into action at this stage, using their design skills to get across the core of an

Getting the most out of this book...

1 [**Keywords**] > *All the words in square brackets are explained in detail in the glossary.*

3 Colour codes > *A key to the COPIC colour scheme of many of the sample layouts, allowing the images to be recreated accurately.*

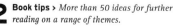

BOOK TIP

Drawing and Designing With Confidence: A Step-By-Step Guide, Mike W. Lin, New York: Van Nostrand Reinhold, 1993

2 Book tips > *More than 50 ideas for further reading on a range of themes.*

idea in the most effective way. Yet even a comprehensive layout should concentrate on the crux of the idea, which is then given its final form in production with the help of photographers, illustrators or filmmakers. And that's the end for even the most beautiful of layouts. It disappears into a drawer, a folder or a file and fades into insignificance, whereas its glorious successors – the ad, poster, brochure or packaging – go on to decorate the walls of agencies and studios in fancy frames.

Concentrate on what really matters. Professional layout artists always restrict themselves to the essentials. That means: think first, then draw. Only those who understand what makes an idea good, original and unmistakable also know what needs to be shown and how.

We will use the many examples in this book to show how easy it is to present a wide variety of themes and ideas, what is most important in rendering them visually and what can be safely left out. We will show the tools you can use to develop professional layouts and how to work quickly and effectively. We will provide tips from experienced professional designers and plenty of useful ideas. We hope that our brief explanations and thematic digressions are fun and inspire you into action. We will show how students using our methods were able to visualize their ideas within a short space of time. And of course we will present a whole string of examples taken from the everyday lives of professionals and successful agencies who, despite their differing styles, all have one thing in common: good ideas. **And now – it's time to get to work!**

4 **Tips and tricks >** *Useful hints to help you get better results and avoid mistakes.*

Speedlines can clarify, signal the unexpected, emphasize emotions or bring flat surfaces to life. It's up to you to decide what role you want them to play.

6 **Ready-to-use >** *A sample storyboard template for you to photocopy, reduce or enlarge. Page 195.*

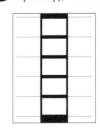

5 **Before and after >** *Examples that help you avoid the most obvious errors. Pages 196–199.*

The right pen for every line.

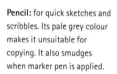

Pencil: for quick sketches and scribbles. Its pale grey colour makes it unsuitable for copying. It also smudges when marker pen is applied.

[COPIC Multiliner SP]: an inking pen available in nine different widths, refillable and with replaceable nibs. Its fine lines will not smudge even when coloured with markers.

[COPIC Multiliner SP Brush]: a medium point that produces soft lines with attractive line variation, depending on how much pressure is applied when drawing.

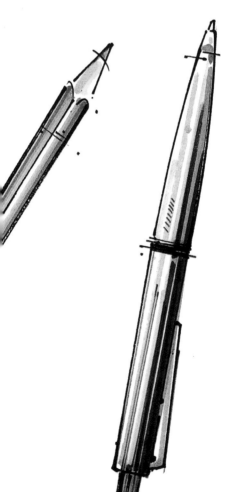

BOOK TIPS

Pencil Sketching, Thomas C. Wang, New York: Van Nostrand Reinhold, 1977

Product Rendering with Markers, Mark Arends, New York: Van Nostrand Reinhold, 1989

On these pages, the same motif is used to illustrate variations in line. Each drawing tool or pen has its own characteristics, creating a range of different effects: fine, medium or broad, full or half tone, hard or soft. Only you can decide which is most suitable for your design and what you find best to work with. Experiment with them all; good art shops have pens and paper you can try out.

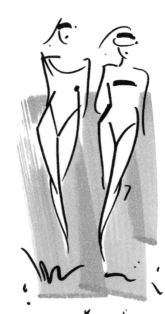

[COPIC Sketch]: brush-like, very soft outlines, well suited to figure drawing and organic lines. Not recommended for drawing technical objects.

[COPIC Marker Broad]: the wider tip of this marker produces full, broad lines for areas of colour or outlines in large-format layouts.

[COPIC Marker Fine]: the thin tip of this dual-ended marker is good for coloured doodles and is effective when used in combination with the broader nib of the pen.

[COPIC Wide]: with a 21mm-wide nib, it's ideal for quick filling of large areas of surface colour and for creating dynamic backgrounds. Like all COPIC markers, it is refillable; the nib can also be replaced.

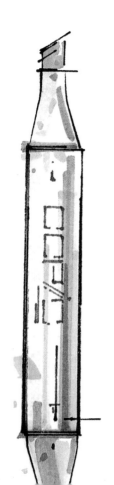

Professional tools for a professional job

Images can be created with all kinds of writing or drawing implements. With its complete system of markers, fineliners and tools, COPIC provides successful professionals with everything they need to produce really exciting designs. [COPIC Markers] come in 214 colours which can be individually blended and refilled. A range of replaceable marker nibs is also available.

Alcohol-based markers are ideal for copying; they don't smudge and are quick to use. The result is a stunning layout that will support any proposal, bringing your ideas to life with conviction.

Replaceable nibs make [COPIC Markers] a universal tool. Line thickness and appearance can be changed in an instant.

However large your colour scheme, COPIC has just what you need.

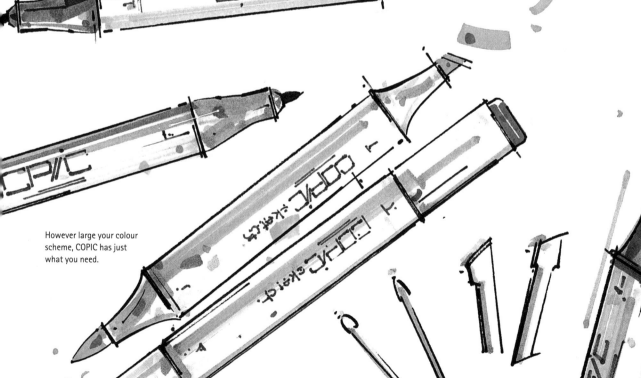

The wide range of [**COPIC Multiliners**] lets you draw lines of any thickness you want.

[
B O O K   T I P

COPIC Marker System
online catalogue:
www.copicmarker.com
]

Sturdy strips of card make the best rulers when working with markers, as the cardboard edge absorbs any excess ink. With rulers made of wood or plastic, the ink stays wet and smudges the next time the ruler is used. This can be very annoying!

[**Opaque White**], scalpel, scissors and masking tape are part of any professional toolkit. And no graphic designer should be without the right [**spray adhesive**] for mounting.

Layouts can be done on any kind of paper. Best of all is specialist layout paper, which is available in different weights. Layout paper is brilliant white, showing the marker colours to best advantage. It is relatively transparent, meaning it can be used for tracing. It also has a bleedproof coating on one side, so that the marker ink will not bleed through onto the sheets below.

Rendering paper is used mainly by product designers and is double-coated, so that both sides can be drawn on, allowing the colours to show through the paper and create delicate effects. But try other kinds of paper and you'll be surprised by the differences in line and colour you can achieve: copying paper, tracing paper, watercolour paper, paper napkins, newsprint, coloured paper or card. These pages will whet your appetite for experiment.

¹⁴ Putting it down on paper

Layout paper: colours stay very bright and edges remain sharp. The paper has a special coating so ink won't soak through quickly. The lightest weight of layout paper is good for cutting and pasting.

Layout paper has a special bleedproof coating on one side so that the marker ink will not go through. With normal paper, bleeding will happen quickly, but that does not mean that it can't be used effectively.

Copier paper: colours come out very strongly but have a tendency to bleed. The edges of coloured areas are therefore hard to control. Ink also seeps easily through the paper's pores. This technique can however be used to achieve fabric-like effects.

Warning: on the reverse side of layout paper (which feels smoother), colours come out paler and with a grainy texture. Ink takes longer to dry on this side, and smears more easily.

When corrections or inlays have been done, the white edges of pasted pieces of paper can sometimes stand out in the montage. If these spoil the overall effect, colour in the white edges carefully.

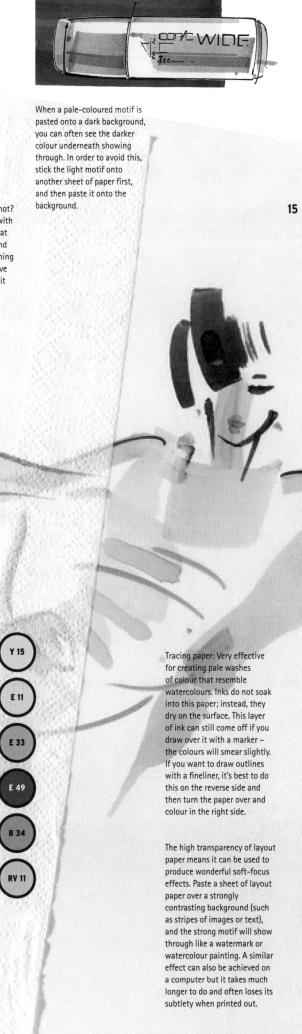

Watercolour paper: Very porous paper that absorbs ink well. Strokes stand out lightly and the grain of the paper shows through. Gives drawings a strong illustrative quality.

A paper napkin: well, why not? It is worth experimenting with all sorts of paper to see what effects they have on line and colour. With copying, scanning and pasting, you can achieve lots of unusual effects. Try it and see.

When a pale-coloured motif is pasted onto a dark background, you can often see the darker colour underneath showing through. In order to avoid this, stick the light motif onto another sheet of paper first, and then paste it onto the background.

Y 15

E 11

E 33

E 49

B 34

RV 11

Another tip for working: leave layout paper in a block until you're done – don't tear out the sheet and cut it down to size until it's all finished. It's much easier to work with the paper still on its pad, because it means you have a little table that you can turn around until it's in the drawing position that suits you. It's also easier to trace or to fill in backgrounds. It's harder to work on a layout with just a single sheet of paper because single sheets are less stable and can be damaged more easily.

Tracing paper: Very effective for creating pale washes of colour that resemble watercolours. Inks do not soak into this paper; instead, they dry on the surface. This layer of ink can still come off if you draw over it with a marker – the colours will smear slightly. If you want to draw outlines with a fineliner, it's best to do this on the reverse side and then turn the paper over and colour in the right side.

The high transparency of layout paper means it can be used to produce wonderful soft-focus effects. Paste a sheet of layout paper over a strongly contrasting background (such as stripes of images or text), and the strong motif will show through like a watermark or watercolour painting. A similar effect can also be achieved on a computer but it takes much longer to do and often loses its subtlety when printed out.

Marker layouts have more impact when areas of the paper are left blank. Totally smothering the paper in ink looks unprofessional. Let the paper work with you.

Building a professional colour palette is surprisingly simple. The COPIC system boasts over 214 different colours, but you won't need to use all of them – just select the ones that are best for you, adding and mixing colours as required. Generally, 30 to 40 markers will be enough: start with red, yellow, green, blue and brown as the basic tones, for lightening and shading. To this, add a sequence of warm and cold greys with five shades apiece and several intermediate colours and pastel tones. It is important that all the colour tones harmonize and produce strong contrasts. If this sounds too complicated, a COPIC 36-colour basic set is available. All COPIC markers can be refilled with ink, making them great to work with.

Brighten up your work with a rainbow of colours

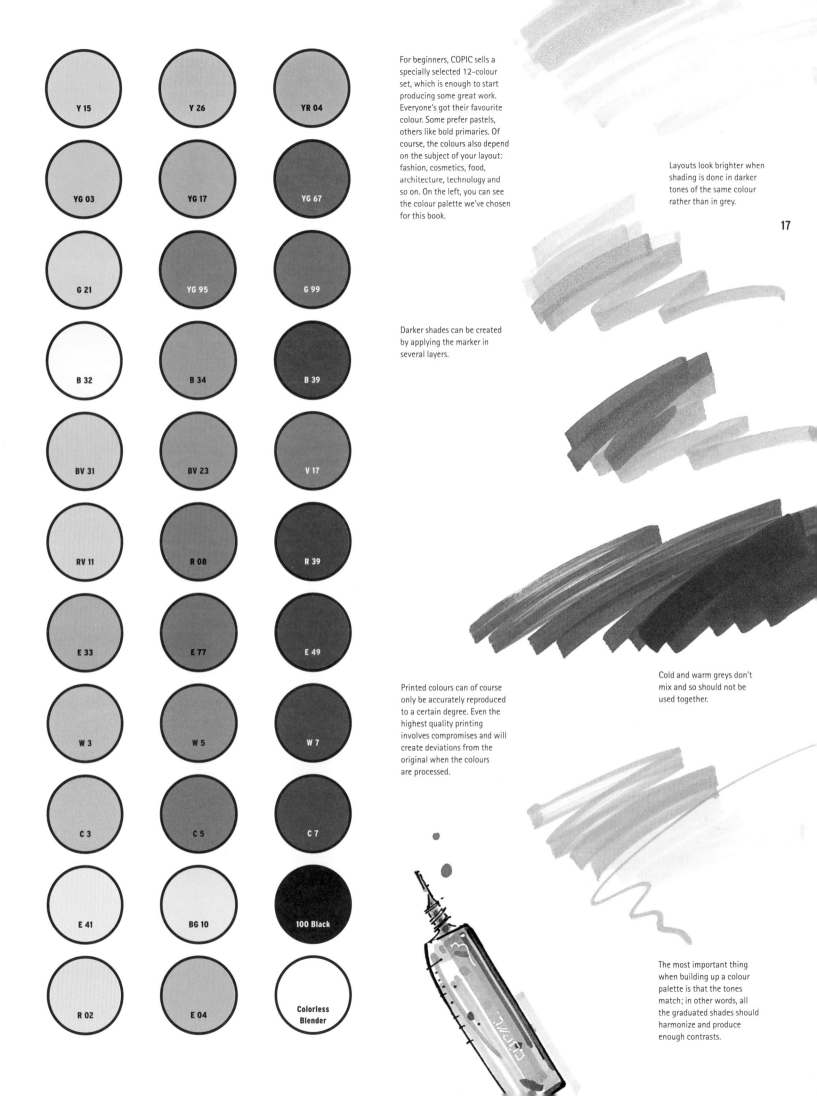

Y 15

Y 26

YR 04

YG 03

YG 17

YG 67

G 21

YG 95

G 99

B 32

B 34

B 39

BV 31

BV 23

V 17

RV 11

R 08

R 39

E 33

E 77

E 49

W 3

W 5

W 7

C 3

C 5

C 7

E 41

BG 10

100 Black

R 02

E 04

Colorless Blender

For beginners, COPIC sells a specially selected 12-colour set, which is enough to start producing some great work. Everyone's got their favourite colour. Some prefer pastels, others like bold primaries. Of course, the colours also depend on the subject of your layout: fashion, cosmetics, food, architecture, technology and so on. On the left, you can see the colour palette we've chosen for this book.

Darker shades can be created by applying the marker in several layers.

Printed colours can of course only be accurately reproduced to a certain degree. Even the highest quality printing involves compromises and will create deviations from the original when the colours are processed.

Layouts look brighter when shading is done in darker tones of the same colour rather than in grey.

Cold and warm greys don't mix and so should not be used together.

The most important thing when building up a colour palette is that the tones match; in other words, all the graduated shades should harmonize and produce enough contrasts.

Keeping it simple

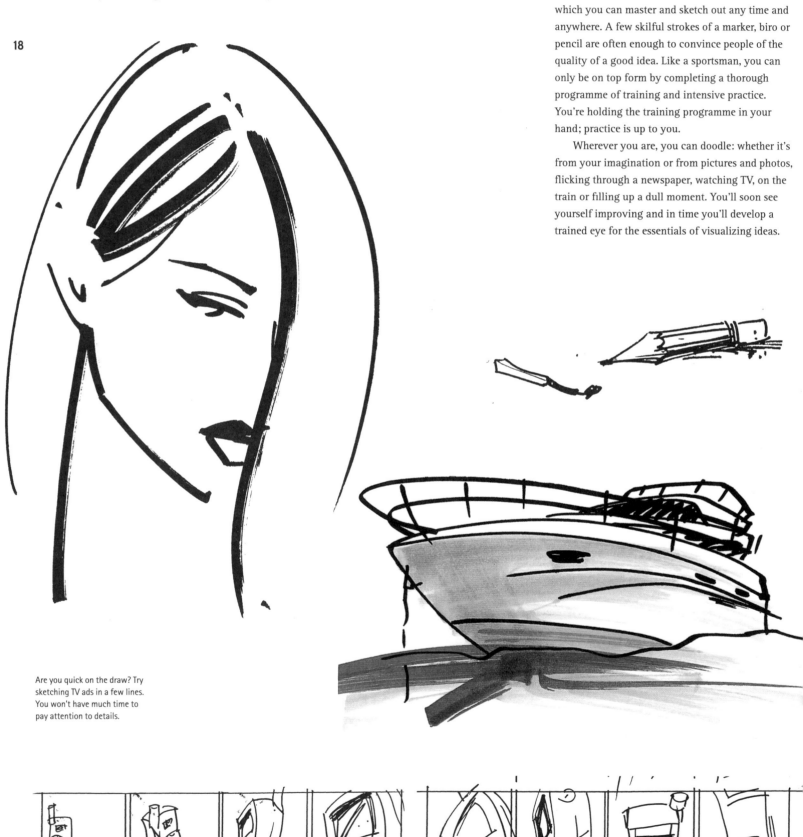

When you want to put your ideas down on paper quickly, you don't only need to know what you want to depict but also what its most important features are. Doodle your way to freedom and build up the courage to illustrate anything – however tricky the subject – in a simple and accessible way.

We're not talking about finished masterpieces here, just the basic crux of your idea. Use simple short cuts and allusions that everyone understands, which you can master and sketch out any time and anywhere. A few skilful strokes of a marker, biro or pencil are often enough to convince people of the quality of a good idea. Like a sportsman, you can only be on top form by completing a thorough programme of training and intensive practice. You're holding the training programme in your hand; practice is up to you.

Wherever you are, you can doodle: whether it's from your imagination or from pictures and photos, flicking through a newspaper, watching TV, on the train or filling up a dull moment. You'll soon see yourself improving and in time you'll develop a trained eye for the essentials of visualizing ideas.

Are you quick on the draw? Try sketching TV ads in a few lines. You won't have much time to pay attention to details.

You can jot down both people and things on paper in a few strokes of a pen. There's no need to be afraid of any subject; all objects have a basic structure and typical shapes. It's up to you to find out what these are and retain this information for later.

BOOK TIPS

Cartooning the Head and Figure, Jack Hamm, New York, Perigee Books, 1982

From Lascaux to Brooklyn, Paul Rand, New Haven: Yale University Press, 1996

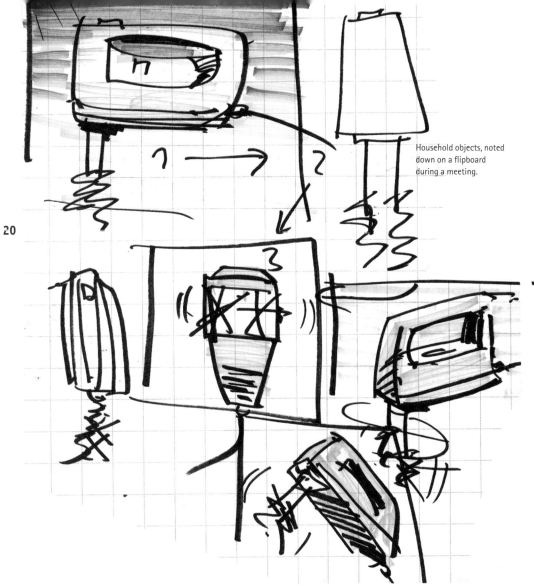

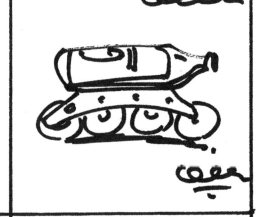

Household objects, noted
down on a flipboard
during a meeting.

Home or away:
you can doodle anywhere

Quick pencil sketches on a
sheet of newspaper, capturing
images of beach life.

A useful loosening-up exercise for students: scribble down the key images from well-known ads. Each image is on show for only 30 seconds, so the essentials have to be copied down quickly.

Jonas Kramer and Sylvia Püchner: doodles done during an exhibition.

BOOK TIPS

Sign and Design, Peter Jenny, Zurich: Institute of Visual Design, 1981

Design Media: Techniques for Watercolor, Pen and Ink, Pastel and Colored Marker, Ron Kasprisin, New York: John Wiley, 1999

Anyone familiar with the working routine of creatives, or who knows about the time pressures that freelance illustrators and layout artists have to work under, is well aware that every stage of a job has to be planned as economically as possible. Because the lion's share of the time is spent coming up with good ideas and hunting for ones that are even better, it's understandable that there's relatively little time left for visualizing those ideas. This explains why, at the end of the ideas process, layout artists are under a lot of pressure to get down on paper the great ideas that art directors and other creatives have succeeded in coming up with.

Short and sweet: the layout artist also receives a [brief] on what the client wants – often in the form of a few semi-comprehensible scribbles – and then has to get to work at lightning speed. All-night sessions, working weekends and last-minute jobs are all par for the course in the world of advertising. But if layout artists are bright sparks too, they can be prepared for any working situation. Some come into briefing meetings armed with suitable source material. Experienced layout artists have a wide range of images and their own visual shorthand ready to use – for most subjects, they don't need a model; they simply know what things should look like. A lot of practice, an analytical eye and the gift of grasping the essential nature of things and depicting it makes work easy. They know the characteristics of different materials, the effects that light and shade can give and the moods that colours can create.

If the subject matter is rather more complex – such as a storyboard for instance – then artists often rely on their own personal [scrap file] or other source material. If that doesn't yield anything, they create their own picture sources – even entire film sequences – using digital images, which they can then do wonderful things with. Good layout artists are organized and know which tools and materials allow them to work fastest. Many have their own tips, tricks and techniques to make sure that even the most complicated visuals really shine on paper.

When the preparation is all done, everything is ready to go and the required layout can be finished in a flash. The working stages always stay the same, so layout artists know that the sequence that has worked in the past will keep on working in the future: line, light, colour, depth, and special effects. Then a clean version of the whole layout is pasted up and delivered to the agency – or even scanned and emailed to the client. If the layouts are done directly on a computer, the images can be sent in digital form and can be worked on further at a later stage. Any small corrections that are necessary may be carried out by junior art directors or creatives; in the case of larger alterations or alternative approaches, the layout artist must do the job again. But a well-planned working system means that it's also possible – even with the tightest of deadlines – that everything will work out just fine. And that's what everyone really wants.

Line

Light and shade

Just a few skilful and confident strokes are enough to get an image down on paper. A line-drawn layout signals: here is someone who knows what they want, no procrastination, no hesitation. Whether you choose a view from the side, from above or from below depends entirely on the idea. If the subject is a difficult one, a [scrap file] or other source material can be helpful. If need be, you can do a quick internet search for suitable visual references or take shots of complicated subjects with a digital camera to get the angle you need.

In this version, it's been decided which direction the light is coming from and what is in shadow. Reflections of light and shade make the subject of the picture much clearer. Working from the same original drawing, try out the effect of different light conditions. Even in black and white, the motif will become much more solid.

Professional layouts are drawn with quick, confident lines. Crossing lines look more lively than lines that do not meet, which open up the object.

Slow strokes look uneven and lack confidence.

Avoid redrawing lines.

Layout artists work fast, and no wonder! The basic principles are always the same...

Colour gives a layout atmosphere and emotion. Advertising layouts are usually full of strong colours and special effects. Examples from the fields of product design and architecture put the emphasis on technical shapes and the materials used. Fashion uses lively colours; for make-up, the effect is usually softer. Manga comics require a different colour palette to a stand at a trade fair. Let the subject be the deciding factor.

Depth and perspective are the next stage. Additional elements can be built up gradually, but must fit together harmoniously. If you're working with the [montage technique], take care that the perspective works when the images are combined. Compared to the objects in the foreground, everything in the background should seem distant and more roughly drawn. Lines are less heavy and colours are muted.

BOOK TIPS

Creative Advertising: Ideas and Techniques from the World's Best Campaigns, Mario Pricken, London and New York: Thames & Hudson, 2002

Advertising Today, Warren Berger, London: Phaidon, 2001

Unpublished: Best Rejected Advertising, ed. Manuel Bonik, Berlin: Grey Press, 1997–99

Design Presentation: Techniques for Marketing and Project Proposals, Ernest Burden, New York and London: McGraw-Hill, 1992

In storyboards, movement can be introduced with just a few lines. [Speedlines], which will be familiar from comic strips, strengthen the idea of movement and help the viewer get involved. In an [animatic], the idea of motion is added later through image and sound editing. Expensive to produce, but very effective.

Loose layout lines and quick colouring

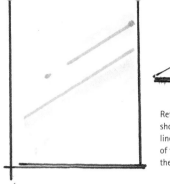

Reflections on flat surfaces should be drawn with diagonal lines, not parallel with the edge of the paper. This emphasizes the light source and adds depth.

Smooth surfaces are suggested by using reflections. The strength or lightness of these depends on the material. Draw reflection lines diagonally, taking them right from one side of an object to the other.

Use straight lines for reflections.

Don't start in the middle. It will look like someone's been cleaning windows!

Whether they are straight, bent or curved, fast lines work best; if they are drawn quickly, they won't become wobbly. Slow lines can be jerky, and easily become shaky and unsure. If you're working quickly and something goes wrong, don't spend a long time correcting your mistake: just start the whole thing over again. Corrected lines will always stand out because they tend to be thicker, and therefore attract the viewer's eye for the wrong reasons.

[B O O K   T I P

The New Complete Illustration Guide, Larry Evans, New York: Van Nostrand Reinhold, 1997]

Professional layouts are drawn with quick, sure lines. When they are, it doesn't really matter if they aren't entirely straight or exact to the millimetre. They only have to be confident. Nobody will let themselves be persuaded by someone who seems unsure.

Filling in colours is easy with markers – a double layer of colour produces a darker shade and makes surfaces more solid. Only use straight lines going in the same direction; criss-crossing lines look messy.

Always fill in objects lengthways; you will need fewer strokes and less line breaks that way.

When drawing woodgrain, make sure that the lines go lengthways and right across. Don't let the grains start or end in the middle of the surface, or it might look more like an infestation of woodworms!

The best way to colour backgrounds is with parallel lines, using a mask. Take the pen off the paper as little as possible, or it might look blotchy. To avoid creating 'steps' around objects, draw an outline first, and then fill.

Lettering: adding text to match your layouts

Headline

Running te

Subhead

Footnote

Whether it's an ad, a poster or a catalogue, most designs involve a combination of picture and text elements. And of course, the text that you use needs to match the style of the layout. At thumbnail stage it's enough to quickly sketch in the headlines and running text. There's no need to go into detail. When the layout is pasted up later, then you can make the headline legible and check that it matches the design. If the text is a key feature, the choice of font is important or the text needs to be legible, then set it all on a computer, print it out and paste it in.

Hilfslinie.

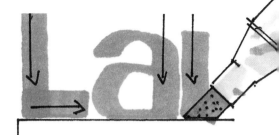

When handlettering, keep the ascenders and descenders quite short, the letters relatively close together, and the line spacing quite tight. It will look neater that way.

No one will mind if you use your own handwriting. But if you're unsure, look at the lettering used in comic books for tips.

Write headlines over a straight edge, to keep them in line. Write with the broad tip of the marker held in the same position, and do not twist it. Make sure that your ruler doesn't slip.

When headlines need to stand out in negative on a dark ground, draw them in positive first. Then use the mask to draw a dark fill around the lettering. Although the lettering will still be in positive, it will look negative against the dark background.

ABC   ABCD

At rough stage, it's usually sufficient to indicate where a headline will be placed or where the running text will fit. A few lines can be used to indicate different kinds of type; large or small, bold or light, justified or unjustified. A mask is invaluable for this.

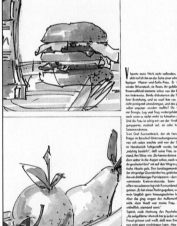

Clear, compact lettering always looks best.

B O O K   T I P

Drawing and Designing With Confidence: A Step-By-Step Guide, Mike W. Lin, New York: Van Nostrand Reinhold, 1993

It's hard to indicate typographical details with a marker pen, but at layout stage it doesn't matter. A rough outline is all that's needed. Anything that progresses to a later stage will be reworked digitally anyway.

Locker schreiben und kompakt – das ist wichtig.

Der einsame Teebeutel.

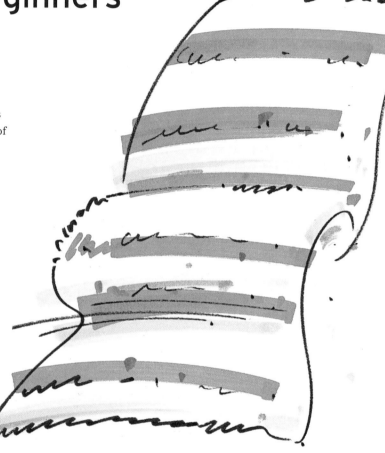

Fabric is soft and can form folds. Thick fabrics, such as wool, are indicated by slight roughness in the surface (fluff).

28

Material science for beginners

All materials are composed differently and have their own properties. This can be indicated in a layout with abstract symbols and short cuts that represent different surfaces. Look closely at objects from now on, and try to notice the characteristics of each material. Of course, there are some short cuts that are quick to use (for example, woodgrain) and others that are not always immediately apparent (for example, pitting on stone surfaces).

You can tell whether short cuts for different materials are sufficiently obvious if they can be applied to geometric objects and the material can still easily recognized. It's much easier to identify a material using a real-life object, such as a screw for metal, rather than a geometric one. So if the material that geometric objects are made of can be identified by sight, this will be even easier when the same effect is applied to a real-life object. Pay careful attention to the characteristics of glass, wood, material, stone and paper, but never forget that these are just helpful symbols and should be used sparingly.

The [bleed-through technique] is useful for depicting porous or rough surfaces. This involves working with markers on normal uncoated paper. The pores in the paper allow some of the marker ink to seep through to the piece lying underneath. This can create surprisingly effective results but should be used sparingly.

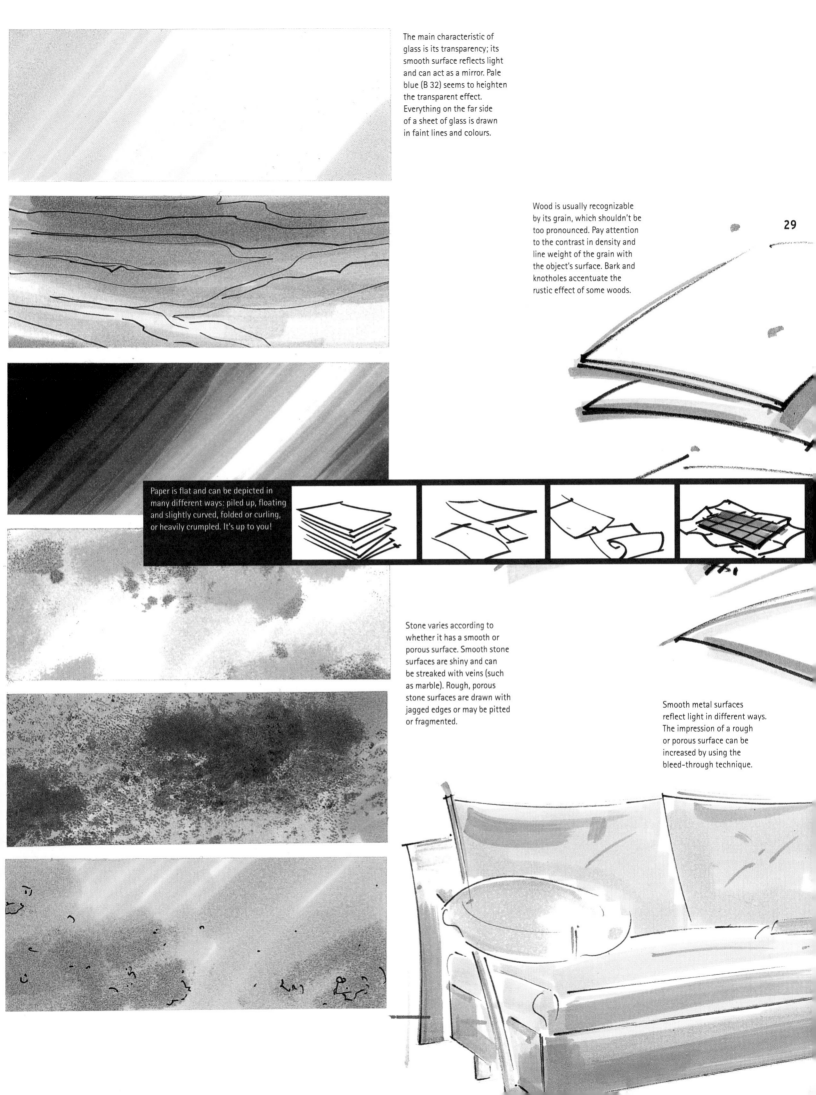

The main characteristic of glass is its transparency; its smooth surface reflects light and can act as a mirror. Pale blue (B 32) seems to heighten the transparent effect. Everything on the far side of a sheet of glass is drawn in faint lines and colours.

Wood is usually recognizable by its grain, which shouldn't be too pronounced. Pay attention to the contrast in density and line weight of the grain with the object's surface. Bark and knotholes accentuate the rustic effect of some woods.

Paper is flat and can be depicted in many different ways: piled up, floating and slightly curved, folded or curling, or heavily crumpled. It's up to you!

Stone varies according to whether it has a smooth or porous surface. Smooth stone surfaces are shiny and can be streaked with veins (such as marble). Rough, porous stone surfaces are drawn with jagged edges or may be pitted or fragmented.

Smooth metal surfaces reflect light in different ways. The impression of a rough or porous surface can be increased by using the bleed-through technique.

A masterly use of materials: metal tubes that reflect light, a TV screen with a reflective surface and an armchair whose hi-tech construction is clearly visible.

What makes fabric soft and stone hard?
Every substance has its own characteristics

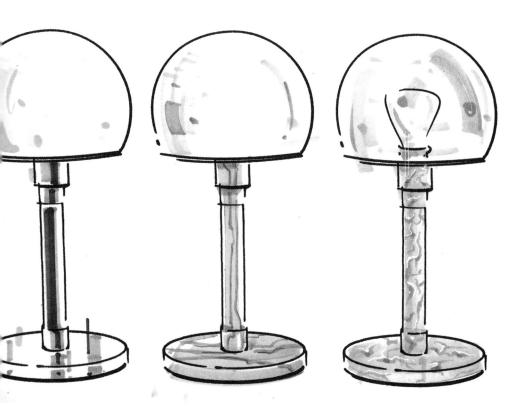

When you're drawing technical or household objects and architectural features, it's particularly important to render materials and their appearance clearly. Quickly drawn lines, timesaving short cuts and suitable colours are just as important as the skilful use of light and shade. Light produces interesting colour modulations and brings a layout to life. Don't forget: white paper enhances contrasts, so avoid cluttering the paper. A hint of colour is usually enough to get the concept across; our own visual memories and experiences will fill in the blanks.

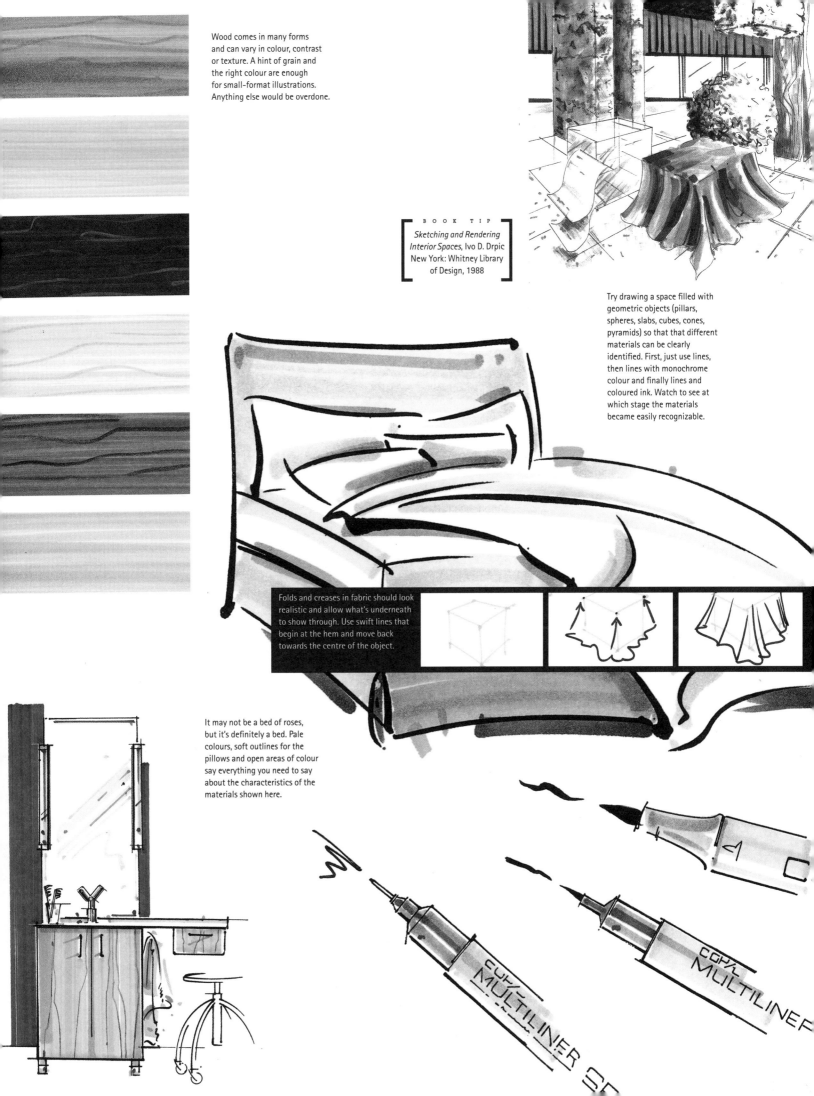

Wood comes in many forms and can vary in colour, contrast or texture. A hint of grain and the right colour are enough for small-format illustrations. Anything else would be overdone.

B O O K   T I P
Sketching and Rendering Interior Spaces, Ivo D. Drpic
New York: Whitney Library of Design, 1988

Try drawing a space filled with geometric objects (pillars, spheres, slabs, cubes, cones, pyramids) so that that different materials can be clearly identified. First, just use lines, then lines with monochrome colour and finally lines and coloured ink. Watch to see at which stage the materials became easily recognizable.

Folds and creases in fabric should look realistic and allow what's underneath to show through. Use swift lines that begin at the hem and move back towards the centre of the object.

It may not be a bed of roses, but it's definitely a bed. Pale colours, soft outlines for the pillows and open areas of colour say everything you need to say about the characteristics of the materials shown here.

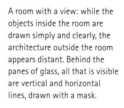

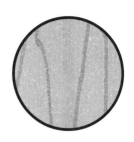

A room with a view: while the objects inside the room are drawn simply and clearly, the architecture outside the room appears distant. Behind the panes of glass, all that is visible are vertical and horizontal lines, drawn with a mask.

Mastering materials:
you'll soon be living the high life

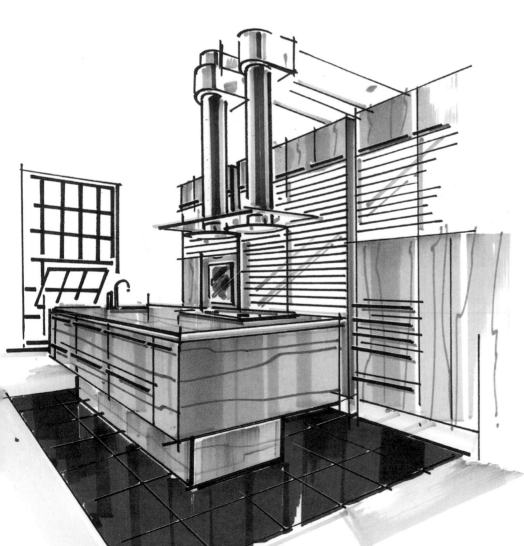

Another version of the scene shown in the main image opposite, but this time completely redrawn with heavier lines. The thick strokes of colour were all done with the broad tip of a [COPIC Wide] marker. When several strokes are laid on top of each other, the surfaces soon start to shine.

An example of technology and materials coming together. This modern fitted kitchen is brought to life by the combination of materials and subtle reflections of light. This sort of work can't be done without a [mask]. The pale grain on the dark wood and the light reflections were added later using a pastel crayon or [COPIC Opaque White]. The dark floor tiles were drawn separately and pasted in. Note the way that the criss-crossing lines accentuate the hi-tech theme.

C 5
C 7
B 32
B 34
B 14
E 13

BOOK TIP
Perspective Without Pain, Phil Metzger, Cologne and London: Taschen, 1997

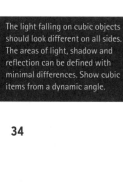
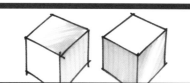

34

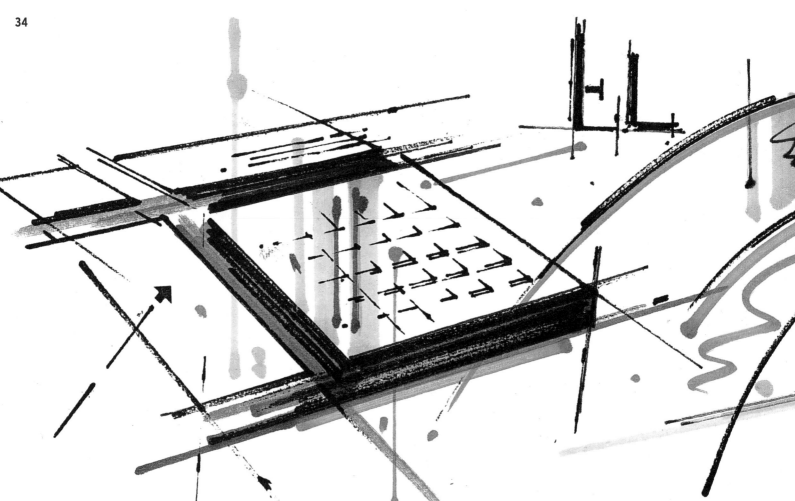

Technology needs to look technical

The following tips will bring your technical layouts to life:
- Quickly drawn lines stop layouts from looking clumsy and lifeless.
- Avoid combining different thicknesses of line within the same layout.
- Draw smooth curves without bumps or blotches. You don't want your product to look like a reject.
- Avoid wobbly lines, short strokes and overdrawing. It always shows.
- Use the right combination of ruled and freehand lines.

- Vary the amount of pressure in your lines; this can increase the illusion of depth.
- Make objects look solid by using quick lines that cross slightly.
- Avoid leaving corners open.
- Accentuate lines by deliberately pausing at the end, to make the endpoint heavier.
- Only use reflections if they won't distract from the overall effect.
- Make sure that reflections on curved surfaces are positioned correctly.

- Make sure that your style stays consistent in both small- and large-format illustrations.
- Objects that are difficult to draw from memory can be copied from a [scrap file].
- Borrow only the key features when copying from picture sources.
- Draw objects that will have continuous backgrounds or vignettes separately and then paste them in.

Technological objects are planned, designed and produced using technical tools. Therefore the way that we choose to depict this specific subject area should also be technically orientated. There are tools that can be used to create outlines, shapes, reflections, harsh edges and coloured surfaces. [Masks] and [templates] can be useful aids, as straight or parallel lines are almost impossible to draw freehand. This reduces the risk of making mistakes and having to redraw everything. And because most layout artists think practically, they like to remove unnecessary elements of risk from their work. Tools aside, however, what brings a

professional layout to life is dynamic, confidently drawn lines. It's crucial to make sure that freehand lines and those drawn using aids are successfully combined. A layout should whet your appetite for the product to come, and a sterile lifeless image won't allow this to happen. Even when the theme is technology, the layout is still the visualization of an idea, so tools should only be used when you want to avoid taking artistic risks (for example, for drawing long parallel lines, strong reflections, concentric circles or rows of identical objects). Try everything else freehand with lots of energy; it's more fun, saves time and gives any layout the lift that it needs.

BOOK TIP
The Illustrated Room,
Vilma Barr, New York:
McGraw-Hill, 1997

35

A mask is a useful tool when you need very straight lines (e.g. for reflections). It should be made of stiff cardboard, should not have a frayed or ragged edge, and should fit neatly in the hand. If the edge gets dirty, cut it off.

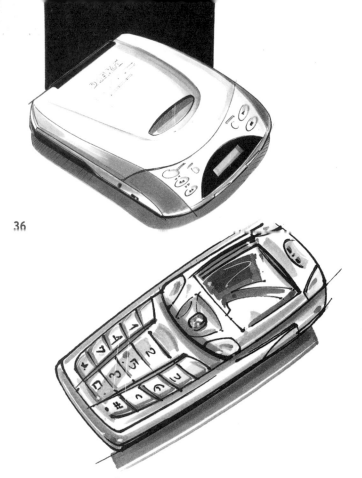

When a technical object is well known and easy to recognize, you have plenty of scope for variation. This collection of impressive layouts from Wiesbaden students showcases a range of different styles. However, the answering machine (Dennis Nussbaum), shaver and storyboard (Jens Hartmann) do have one thing in common; they clearly convey the theme of technology and are quickly drawn.

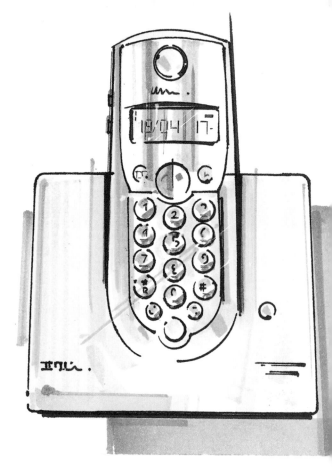

Mobile phones have many small surfaces, but they benefit from skilfully placed reflections and an accurate depiction of features such as the keypad, numbers and display screen.

Bringing technology to life

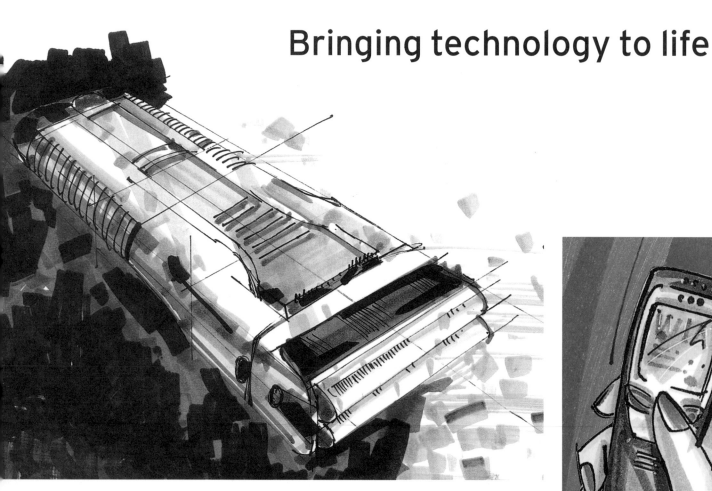

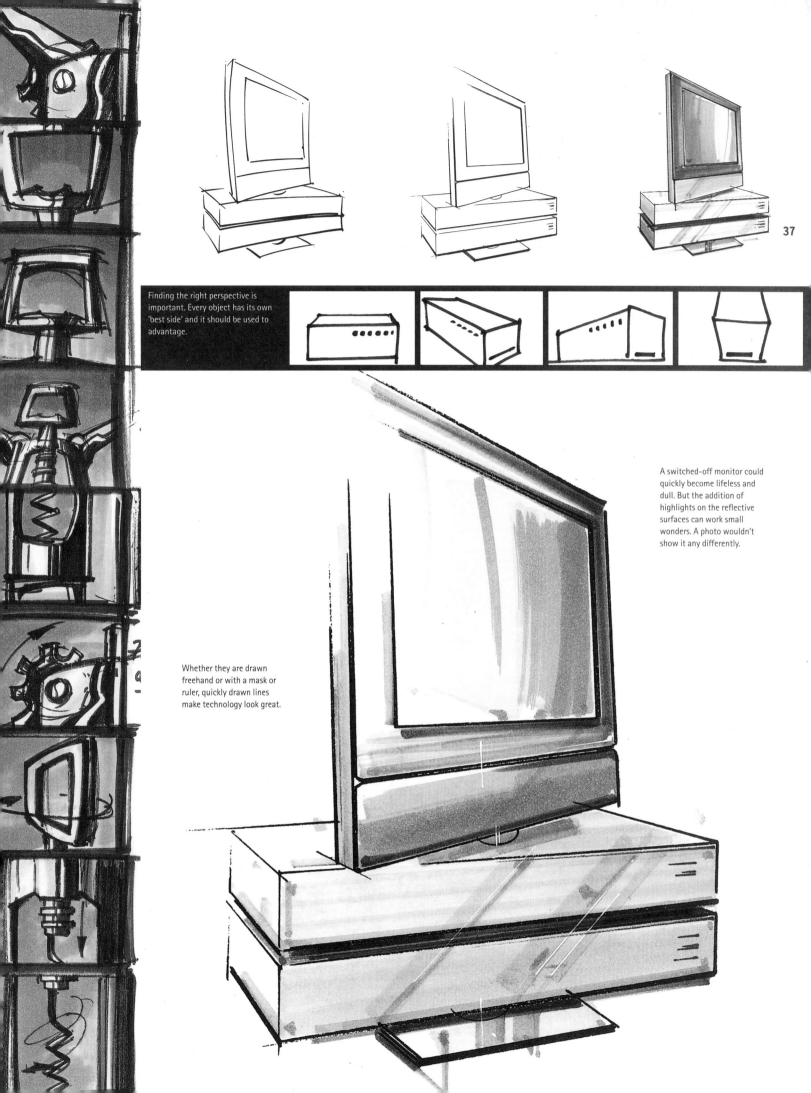

Finding the right perspective is important. Every object has its own 'best side' and it should be used to advantage.

A switched-off monitor could quickly become lifeless and dull. But the addition of highlights on the reflective surfaces can work small wonders. A photo wouldn't show it any differently.

Whether they are drawn freehand or with a mask or ruler, quickly drawn lines make technology look great.

Earlier we learnt that every material has its own characteristics, which are recognizable even when applied to geometric objects. If the object is rendered clearly, then this makes things much easier. A screw, for example, is immediately recognizable by its shape, thread or metallic colour. It doesn't take much to make an object identifiable, as long as the basics are right. If objects not only need to be identifiable but also need to appear three-dimensional, suggesting space which isn't there, then we need light. We will now demonstrate how to draw an object in the right light with this red screwdriver.

1. First, draw the outline of the object using a combination of ruled and freehand lines. If you try to draw the entire object freehand, you will soon discover that it's extremely difficult to draw the long, straight lines in parallel. But with a card mask, it is no problem. Using a mask is also the best way of drawing with variations in line pressure. The lines themselves then appear three-dimensional.

2. Apply the base colour with a marker, leaving out white reflective areas. This is easier if you use a mask.

3. Build up shading by adding matching darker tones. Don't forget to observe how the light falls on the object.

RV 11

R 08

R 39

C 3

B 32

A matter of practice

Technical objects have more impact when the colour tones have as much contrast as possible. This gives the layout punch, effectively emphasizing the product.

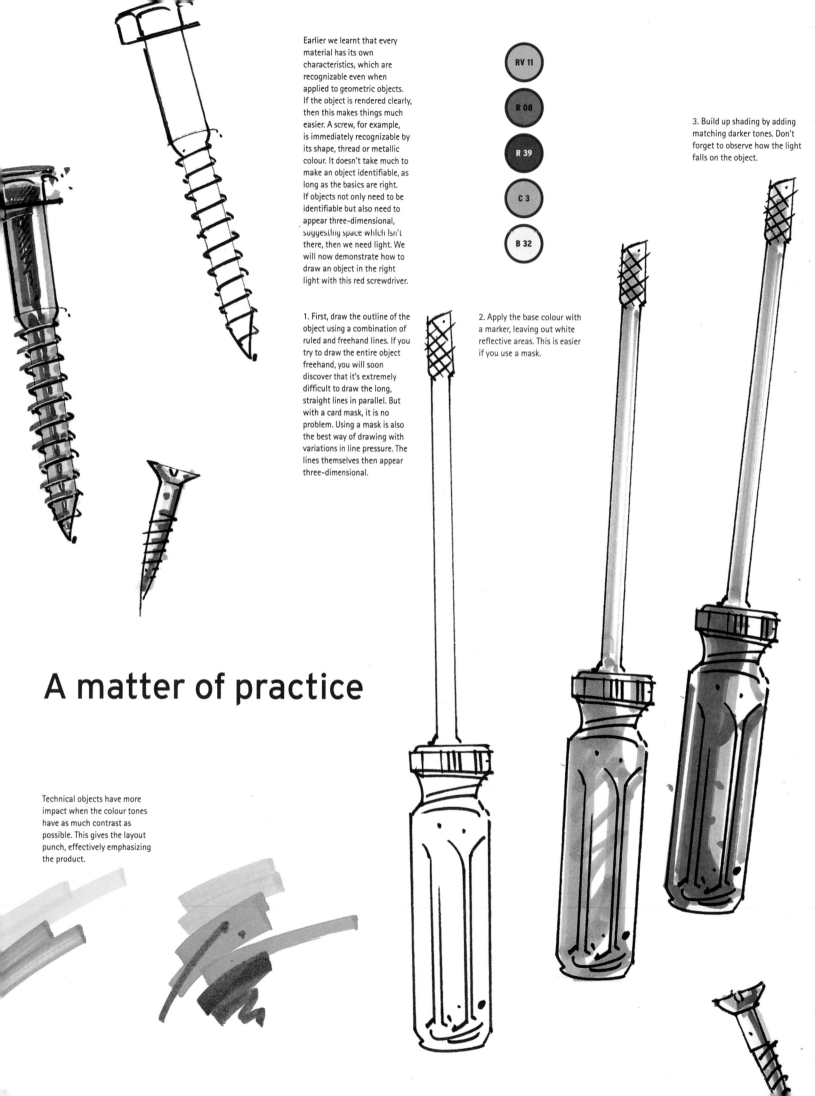

4. Now the colour contrast and three-dimensionality are increased by adding even darker colours. Prominent areas are touched up with highlight ink. You can use [**Opaque White**] or correction fluid for this, or scrape in the highlights with a scalpel.

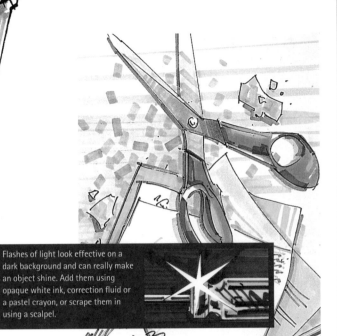

Flashes of light look effective on a dark background and can really make an object shine. Add them using opaque white ink, correction fluid or a pastel crayon, or scrape them in using a scalpel.

Anja Ganster's image (above) shows how a little can say a lot. Quick lines, a carefully planned composition and just the right amount of colour gives a professional effect.

The car stereo below has accurately placed controls and readouts, and seems real enough to touch with its heavy black shadows and highlights. The shading and highlights give an almost photographic effect. The LED display was coloured right at the beginning and the darker shading was then added over the top, allowing the colours to shine through.

This sparkling screwdriver in its dramatically lit setting is by Veronique Noçon. The green tones of the plastic handle make a striking constrast with the dark background and white highlights.

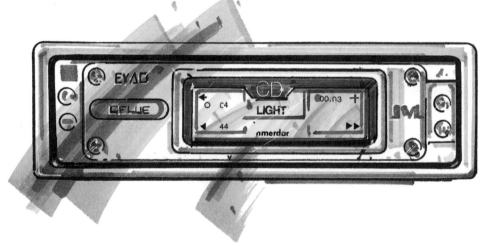

Professionals customize their marker tips by cutting notches into them with a scalpel. Replaceable COPIC nibs are ideal for this. This makes it easy to draw parallel lines – anything from twisted cable to a bowl of spaghetti!

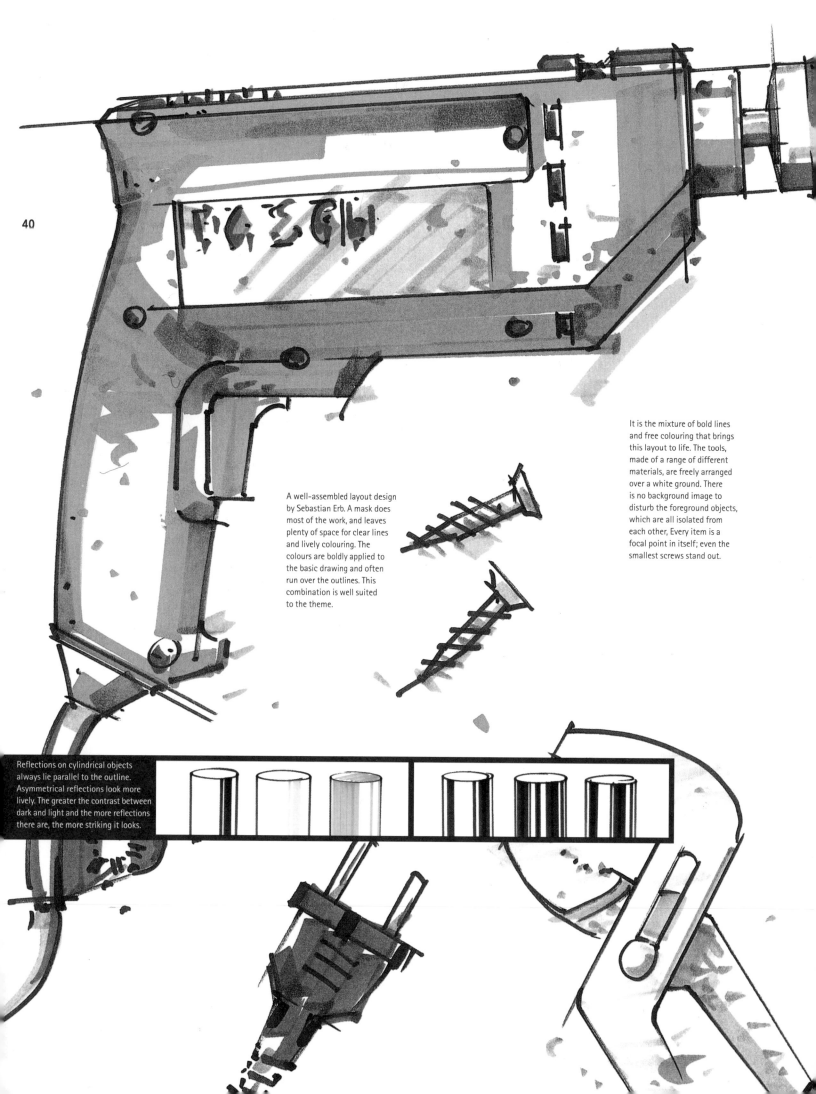

A well-assembled layout design by Sebastian Erb. A mask does most of the work, and leaves plenty of space for clear lines and lively colouring. The colours are boldly applied to the basic drawing and often run over the outlines. This combination is well suited to the theme.

It is the mixture of bold lines and free colouring that brings this layout to life. The tools, made of a range of different materials, are freely arranged over a white ground. There is no background image to disturb the foreground objects, which are all isolated from each other, Every item is a focal point in itself; even the smallest screws stand out.

Reflections on cylindrical objects always lie parallel to the outline. Asymmetrical reflections look more lively. The greater the contrast between dark and light and the more reflections there are, the more striking it looks.

Keeping a handle on chaos

Legibility becomes an issue when lots of objects need to be scattered chaotically. Discipline is required to compose a scene that involves objects of different shapes and materials overlapping each other and a range of sizes and perspectives, all on top of a grained wooden background. You can see how important it is to give individual objects bold, solid outlines, and to use clear colour boundaries to divide them up.

41

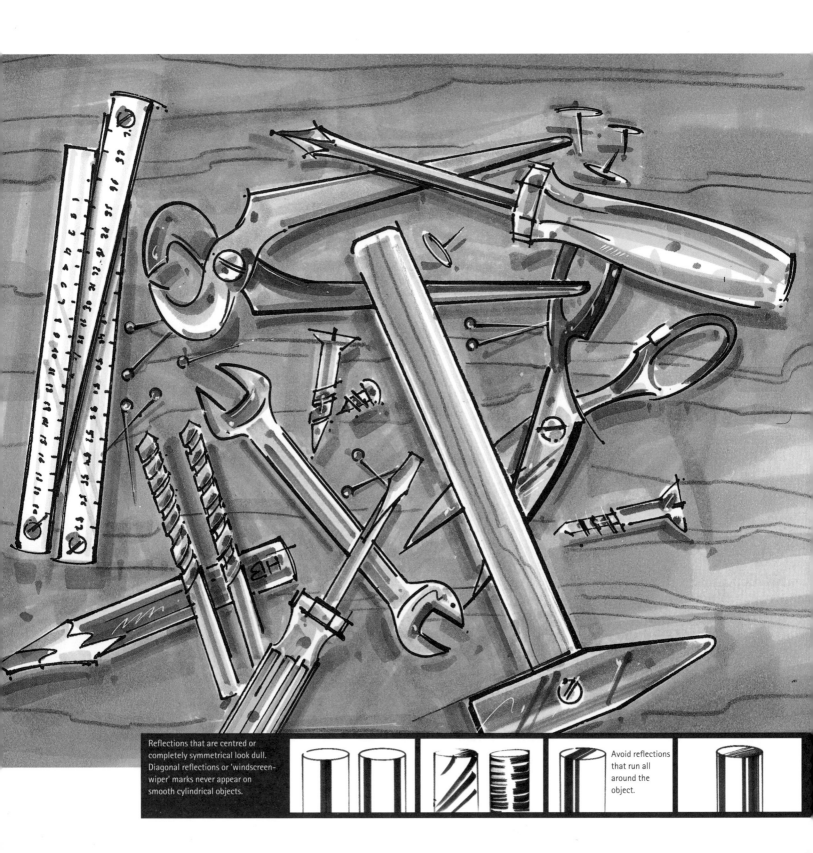

Reflections that are centred or completely symmetrical look dull. Diagonal reflections or 'windscreen-wiper' marks never appear on smooth cylindrical objects.

Avoid reflections that run all around the object.

It's quite normal to have to make corrections to layouts. Sometimes an object looks great, but something about the lighting in the background doesn't work. Or perhaps the art director sees the finished layout and casually comments: 'We'll have to do it all again. The mermaid on page 168 needs to look a lot more seductive.' Of course, you'll want to avoid redoing the whole layout again, because that would take too long, but you don't have to. You can use the inlay technique to make both large and small corrections to your layouts – it's quick to do, and invisible too.

The inlay technique: a basis for experiments and corrections

This layout for this music system was made in three parts. First the object itself, with its technical details and little points of reflected light. Then the table top in dark wood with heavy grain: the illusion of light falling on the surface was created simply by adding a couple of extra areas of colour in the same shade of brown. The background was added last, and was carefully cut out with a scalpel from around the object. After the pieces were pasted up, any white edges of cut paper were smoothed down with a thumbnail so that they didn't stand out. Why work this way? To convince the clients that the dark background they wanted is too dominant, and that the product looks better against a white background.

E 29

B 32

B 34

Y 15

YR 04

RV 11

C 7

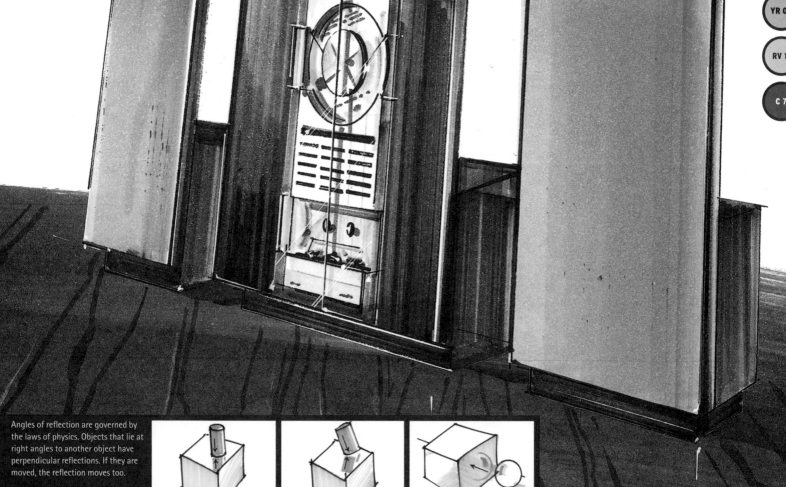

Angles of reflection are governed by the laws of physics. Objects that lie at right angles to another object have perpendicular reflections. If they are moved, the reflection moves too.

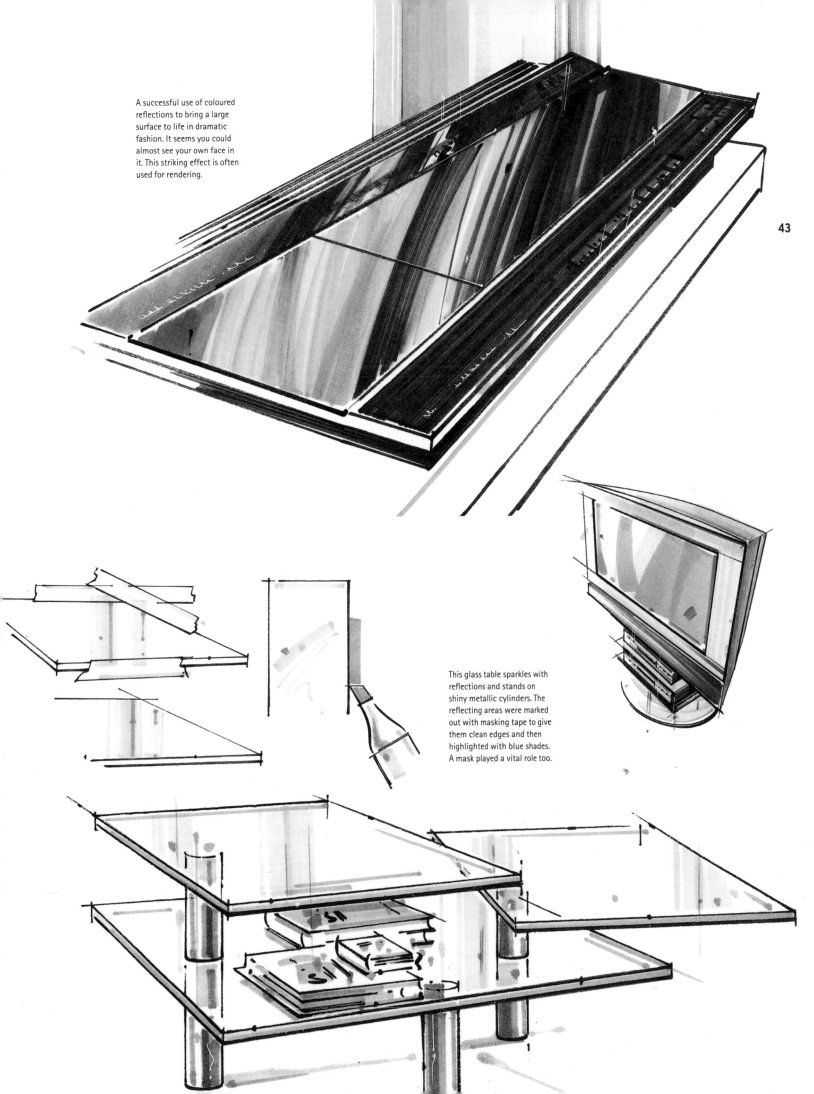

A successful use of coloured reflections to bring a large surface to life in dramatic fashion. It seems you could almost see your own face in it. This striking effect is often used for rendering.

This glass table sparkles with reflections and stands on shiny metallic cylinders. The reflecting areas were marked out with masking tape to give them clean edges and then highlighted with blue shades. A mask played a vital role too.

Reflections are created by light and can be used to indicate different kinds of materials. They alter according to the position of the light source and the object's surface shape.

If you are unsure about how reflections work, try to study objects and their appearance more closely in future.

Wisps of smoke added with a pastel crayon stand out against the dark background.

Along with perspective and overlap, light is the key factor in creating three-dimensionality. As a general rule, the stronger the contrast of light and dark, the greater the illusion of depth will be. The illusion of light can be achieved by using colour shading or in line art through sharp contrasts of black and white. To present your ideas in the right light, it is worth bearing the following points in mind. Is lighting a crucial part of your idea? If so, where is the light coming from? Is it bright or soft? What overall mood does the light source create? Is it warm or cold? Harsh or diffuse? Straight or steeply angled? Does the light source create reflections on the surface of the objects? How does the material depicted react to light?

If you can't decide, try making small sketches to test different effects of light and shade. This dispel any doubts and help you to make the right decisions before moving on to larger designs. Another important point is that you don't need to launch into this topic with scientific precision! A layout is, after all, just a visual expression of an idea and doesn't have to be ultra-realistic. Technical details and the finer points of lighting can be left to the photographer, director or illustrator who will later turn your layout into reality.

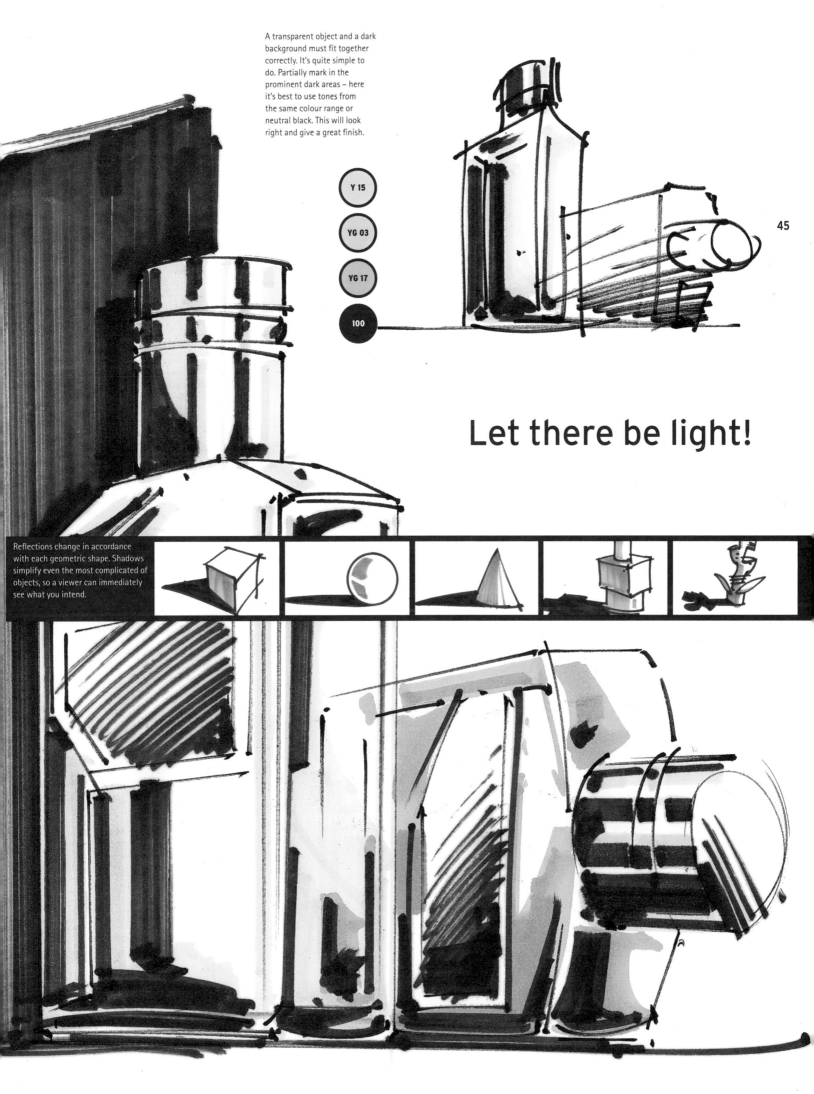

A transparent object and a dark background must fit together correctly. It's quite simple to do. Partially mark in the prominent dark areas – here it's best to use tones from the same colour range or neutral black. This will look right and give a great finish.

Y 15

YG 03

YG 17

100

Let there be light!

Reflections change in accordance with each geometric shape. Shadows simplify even the most complicated of objects, so a viewer can immediately see what you intend.

Design for a display stand with dark, shiny materials and dramatic, effective use of light. The background is partially filled to add depth. This creates contrast without overwhelming the layout.

Showing your product in a professional light

A presentation stand for cosmetics: the subtle colour contrasts of wood and glass are artificially heightened by the addition of a strip of dark background.

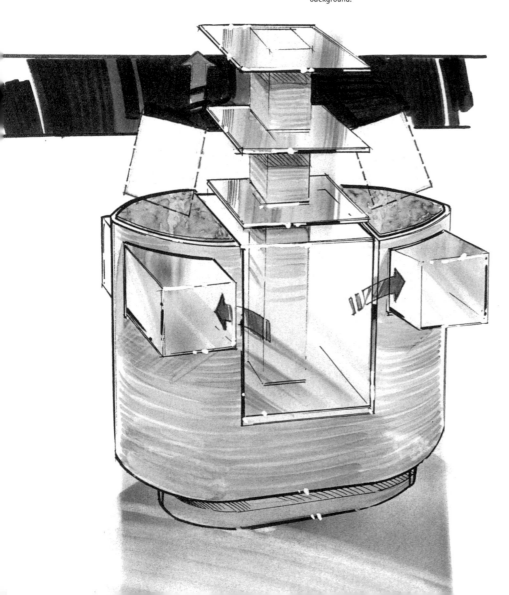

Successful depiction of materials and the way they interact and work together often plays a major role in professional presentations. That's especially true when – as shown on these pages – the objects themselves don't exist as anything other than a wish to show unusual ideas as attractively as possible. Illustrator Thommy Mallmann (www.tomkong.de) specializes in designing product displays and stands for trade shows, events, shops and exhibitions. One of his tasks is to capture the visual qualities of the materials used in a vivid way. The first stage of any layout is to produce sketches based on technical studies or plans. The object's 'best side' must then be found, so it can be shown to advantage.

Dramatic contrasts of light and dark add depth and show off transparency and highlights to best effect. Despite their apparent perfection, these designs are distinguished by quickly drawn lines, use of colour contrasts, heavy emphasis on the qualities of the materials used (especially sparkle and reflection) and a good feel for striking perspective. It all goes to show that without sound knowledge of the way that products are put together, it's hard to capture their structure and material properties in a layout.

Using mixed media – markers, opaque white, chalk and airbrush – Mallmann produces attractive layouts and three-dimensional designs. Many of his layouts are then computer enhanced, allowing him to add new effects, and making it quick and easy to produce digital image files. This is a great advantage when Mallmann is working with international clients, since his work can be sent anywhere in the world in the blink of an eye.

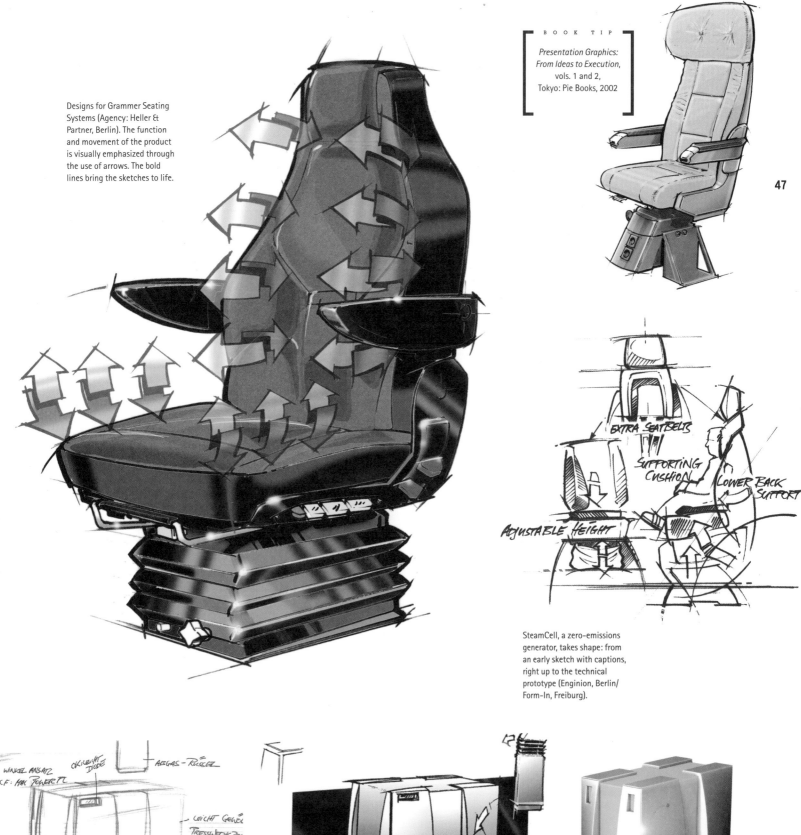

Designs for Grammer Seating
Systems (Agency: Heller &
Partner, Berlin). The function
and movement of the product
is visually emphasized through
the use of arrows. The bold
lines bring the sketches to life.

B O O K   T I P

*Presentation Graphics:
From Ideas to Execution,*
vols. 1 and 2,
Tokyo: Pie Books, 2002

47

EXTRA SEATBELTS

SUPPORTING
CUSHION

LOWER BACK
SUPPORT

ADJUSTABLE HEIGHT

SteamCell, a zero-emissions
generator, takes shape: from
an early sketch with captions,
right up to the technical
prototype (Enginion, Berlin/
Form-In, Freiburg).

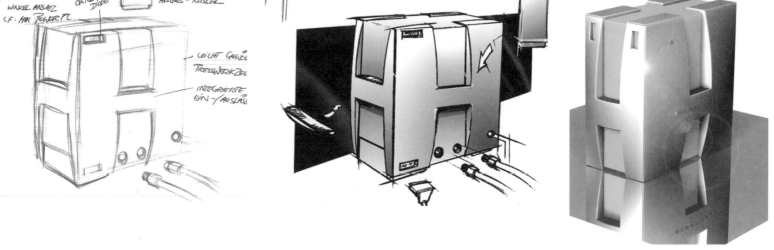

WINKEL ANSATZ
CF: MAC POWERTL

OK-KEUHT
DIODE

ABGAS-RÜSSEL

LEICHT GEWÖL
PRESSWERKZEU

INTEGRIERTE
EIN-/AUSLÄS

A layout in less than ten minutes? That's something worth drinking to!

Above, Markus Remscheid demonstrates how subject and background can work together, and how reflections can add depth. Stark contrasts of light and shade make the green bottle positively sparkle. If you don't believe how many colours there can be in a dark transparent liquid, then try holding a glass of Coca Cola up to the light and look at all the shades you can see.

Objects look better when the endpoints of lines are gently curved to fit together. Keep wineglasses looking delicate by using one line for the stem instead of two.

The step-by-step construction of a still life with transparent objects: the basic line drawing (above), then with added light and shade (centre) and finally, the coloured version against a partial dark ground (below).

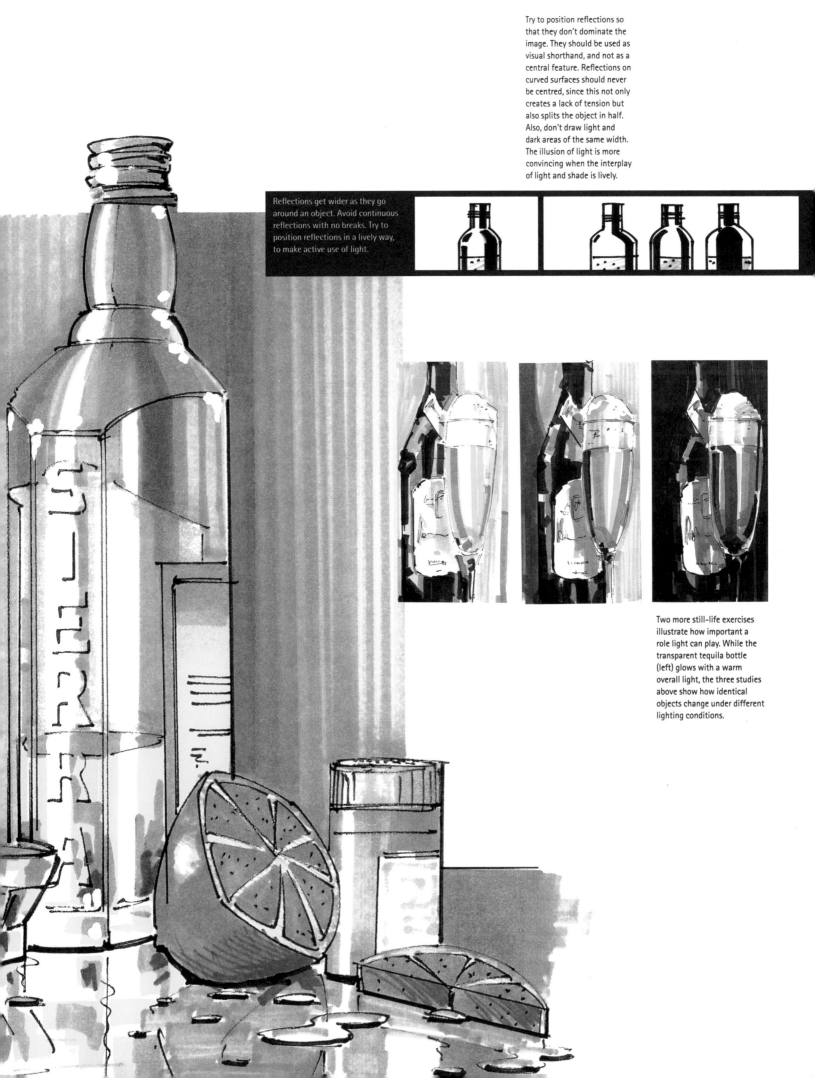

Try to position reflections so that they don't dominate the image. They should be used as visual shorthand, and not as a central feature. Reflections on curved surfaces should never be centred, since this not only creates a lack of tension but also splits the object in half. Also, don't draw light and dark areas of the same width. The illusion of light is more convincing when the interplay of light and shade is lively.

Reflections get wider as they go around an object. Avoid continuous reflections with no breaks. Try to position reflections in a lively way, to make active use of light.

Two more still-life exercises illustrate how important a role light can play. While the transparent tequila bottle (left) glows with a warm overall light, the three studies above show how identical objects change under different lighting conditions.

Food and drink keep body and soul together, or so they say. Professional layout artists know that bright colours and quick lines are the essence of a successful food layout, and work accordingly. So when food is the subject, professionals apply colours that are as pure as possible, and avoid any form of shading that might look dingy. There's no place for grey tones here, and even the number of lines used can be reduced, depending on how light or substantial the subject is meant to look. Pastel shades and large areas of white paper also help to give layouts a fresh flavour. Keep outlines soft, avoiding black if necessary, and replacing it with lighter shades. Use changes in line pressure to emphasize the organic quality of the subject and allow lines to taper off (especially towards the light).

When inking, not everything has to be coloured in exactly. Colour that goes over outlines and beyond them can make a food layout seem natural and bring it to life. Small-format illustrations ignore detail and concentrate on colour accents and structure. Try it out and see how little colour you need to capture the idea of food. A white oval with a yellow dot quickly becomes an egg, a combination of green, red and yellow lines immediately looks like a sandwich, and a tangle of beige lines with red and green dots instantly turns into a pasta dish.

Food layouts that look good enough to eat

This lady obviously knows that what looks good will probably taste good too. These tasty morsels are drawn in just a few lines but can be recognized by anyone. The typical colours of fresh fruit and vegetables mean there can be no doubt about it. Bon appetit!

If your design has to look good enough to eat, you need to use tempting colours. Shading should always be in pure, darker colours, avoiding grey tones.

With complex shapes, focus on the essentials when sketching and use as few lines as possible.

52

A tasty appetizer...

Food layouts look softer
and more natural when the
colour is allowed to spill over
the outlines.

A neutral light blue makes
colours look brighter, so that
even the shadows look tasty.
Avoid using greys.

Usually a few splashes of colour are enough to whet our appetite. As we know, food needs to look good in order to taste good. Layout artists make the most of this, garnishing food spreads with fresh, bright inks. Use matching pure colours for shading.

E 13 E 49 BV 31 B 34 R 39

Fast food or home cooking? Especially in this case you might ask: 'Why go to the bother of drawing a layout – particularly one that's copied from a printed source – when I could just use a colour copier?' Well, you're both right and wrong. If a picture is exactly the way you want it, then there's no point in drawing it again. All you need is a colour photocopier – if you have one to hand. However, you can't always unearth a print-ready photo for everything you need and may have to adapt the ones that you can find. All in all, it's easier to grab your drawing kit and get to work, provided you know what you want. Those who rely on getting their new ideas from flicking through magazines, catalogues and design books shouldn't be surprised if they find themselves regurgitating the same old material. And callouses from turning pages are not exactly one of the better-known traits of a creative genius....

Layouts to make your mouth water

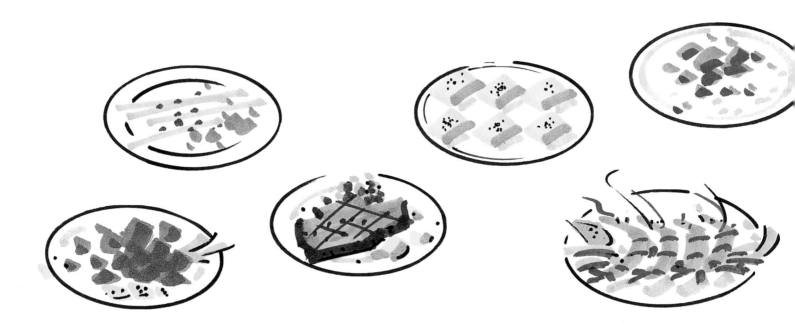

These lively sample spreads were created with the help of images from scrap files. The original composition was copied but all the details were reduced to outlines. It's important to make complex structures and elements as simple as possible and not to become too engrossed with unnecessary details.

Salads, vegetables and side dishes are simply arrangements of coloured shapes, but they should make the viewer's mouth water. While the ingredients form rich areas of colour, the white of the crockery becomes a light background for the finished dish. It's this which makes the food seem so tasty.

Below, Christina Männel uses bright, fresh colours and reduces line contrast by using a brown pen. The brown outline is very subdued in comparison with the other inks. These tempting tidbits use light colours and a high proportion of white.

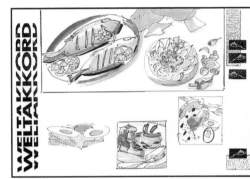

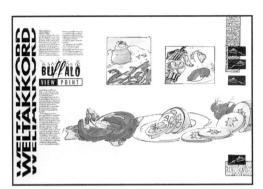

This model seems to have an eye for a healthy snack. Find out how to keep her in shape on page 130.

Which colour combinations remind you of your favourite foods? Try your hand as a visual chef and create your own colourful recipes. You'll be surprised to see how quickly certain colour combinations bring to mind the topic of food.

When it comes to text, our hi-tech friend the Mac makes life much simpler. And it's a good thing too. A layout looks its best with the headline in a font that really suits your campaign. But when you're just doodling, it's seldom worth booting up the computer at the same time – for the simple reason that perfect typesetting is out of place at this stage in the process. Headlines and rough text blocks – and no more than that – are quickly and easily scrawled onto the page with a marker. And don't spend too much time on rendering type with pens or markers. The most you should attempt is a rough distinction between ranged and justified type, sans-serif and serif fonts, and the shapes of the text boxes. So spare yourself the trouble of the rest and look at the examples on page 26.

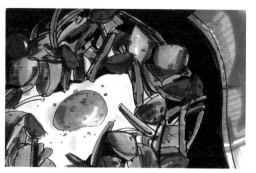

A few lines, the right colours and a generous helping of imagination make the layout below sizzle on the page. Meat, sauce, vegetables and accompaniments stand out clearly. Minimal outlines and lots of white make the layout light, the colours bold – and stomachs rumble. Just tuck in!

Y 15
YR 04
YG 03
YG 17
YG 95
BV 31
B 34
B 32

Add a few dots to season – and dinner's ready!

Cookery for beginners: a side dish of green and red peppers ready in less than a minute.

Fresh fruit by Florian Stucki (below), a stuffed pepper by Sina Preikschat (bottom of page), and a tasty dish from Marloes Kremers (below left): all delicious and ready in just a few minutes.

Here are some food layouts by Wiesbaden students, which were drawn with the help of a **[scrap file]**. Now you may ask 'Why not just photocopy my picture sources and use those for the layout?' Of course you can do this if the borrowed photos are exactly the way you want your layout to be. But often the ingredients are not quite what you need. Perhaps the viewpoint is wrong, or you don't like the setting. And it often takes far too long to find just the right models and adapt them to your new format. If this is the case, you're much better off sketching a quick layout from scratch.

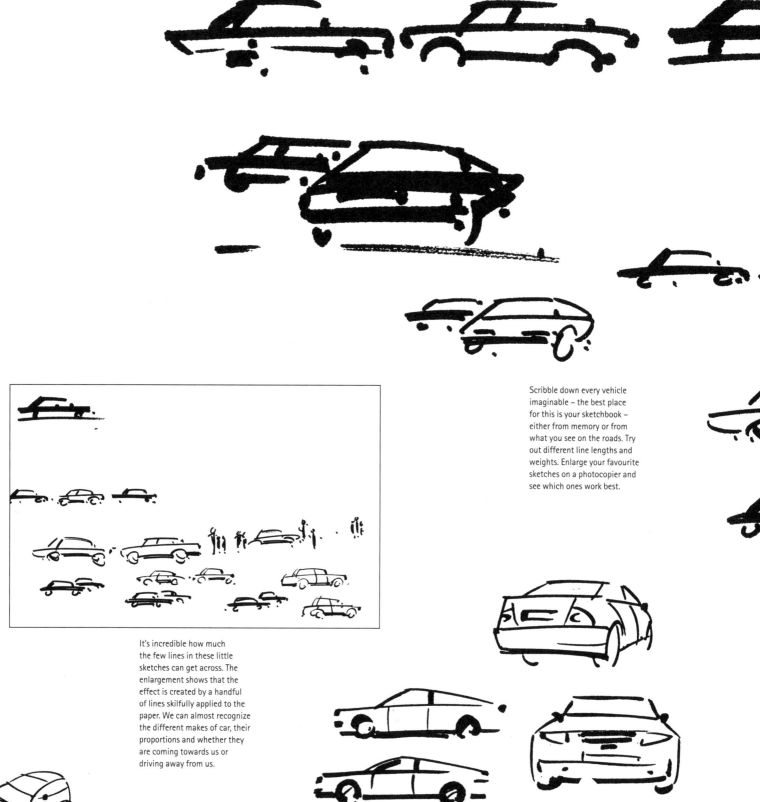

Scribble down every vehicle imaginable – the best place for this is your sketchbook – either from memory or from what you see on the roads. Try out different line lengths and weights. Enlarge your favourite sketches on a photocopier and see which ones work best.

It's incredible how much the few lines in these little sketches can get across. The enlargement shows that the effect is created by a handful of lines skilfully applied to the paper. We can almost recognize the different makes of car, their proportions and whether they are coming towards us or driving away from us.

Car layouts that drive like a dream

Anyone can draw technical objects such as cars in some shape or form. We all see cars every day and can recognize them from far off. This naturally makes them easier to draw. Regardless of whether you're the artist or the observer, a few strokes of the pen are enough to conjure up images of a moving object with four wheels and an engine. To start with, doodle quickly from memory in miniature, then from photos and pictures or from vehicles driving by outside. Compare your sketches to see which ones are clearly recognizable and whether any unnecessary details can be omitted. It won't take you long to discover that greatly simplified sketches with sweeping lines are the most convincing.

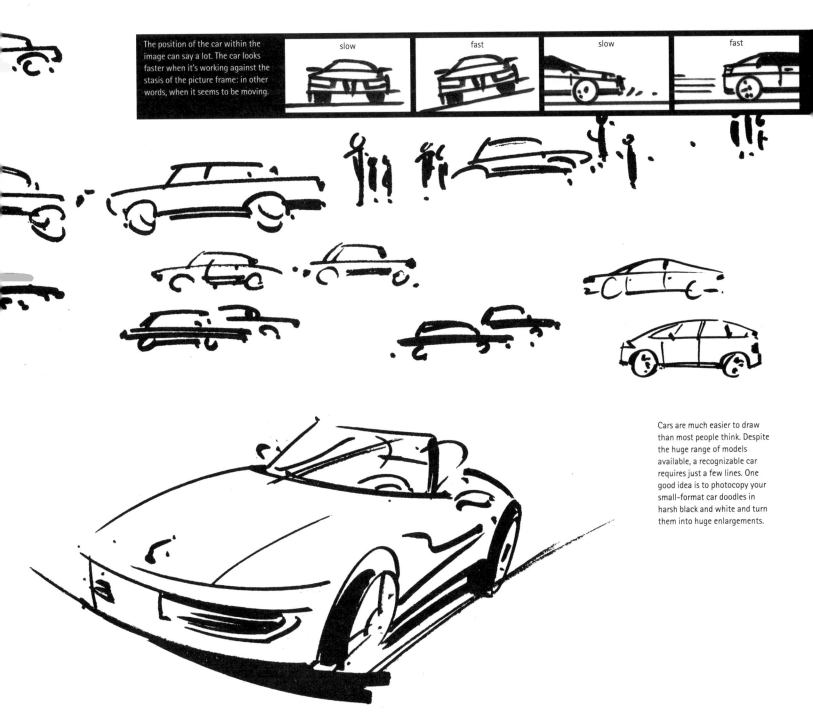

The position of the car within the image can say a lot. The car looks faster when it's working against the stasis of the picture frame: in other words, when it seems to be moving.

slow   fast   slow   fast

Cars are much easier to draw than most people think. Despite the huge range of models available, a recognizable car requires just a few lines. One good idea is to photocopy your small-format car doodles in harsh black and white and turn them into huge enlargements.

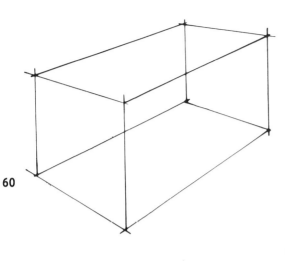

The basics: a box with the approximate proportions of the car, viewed from an interesting perspective.

The object: the proportion and shape of the car are now drawn into the box using a few lines: sporty or chunky, long or short, curved or angled. The edges of the car run parallel with the edges of the box.

Bigger spaces: if you want to show lots of cars together in a larger environment (a city street, car park, motor show or car dealership), simply draw as many boxes as you need. Once these and the other elements in the picture are placed together with the correct perspective, you can follow the steps described for each car.

The details: headlights, radiator grille, bumper, windscreen, door handle and hubcaps are all kept as simple as possible and correctly positioned.

The most difficult part is the wheels, which must lie exactly on the axes. Draw the wheels and hubcaps as flat ellipses with quick strokes. Quick, bold lines prevent the shape of the wheels from getting distorted.

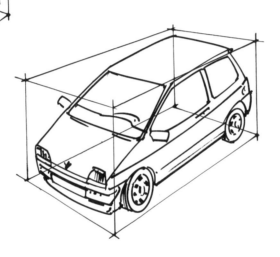

Carving out a car

The axes: since all cars are built symmetrically, the box is very useful as a basis. The axes run parallel to the edges of the box. The wheels stand on the baseline of the construction.

Because the tyres of a car are the hardest part to draw, that's where you should always start. Quick strokes are the only way to draw freehand ellipses properly. Slow lines can easily turn wobbly. If need be, use a template.

With a bit of practice, it's possible to draw flat ellipses freehand. But the nearer the ellipse is to a circle, the more difficult it becomes. The usual solution is to use a [template].

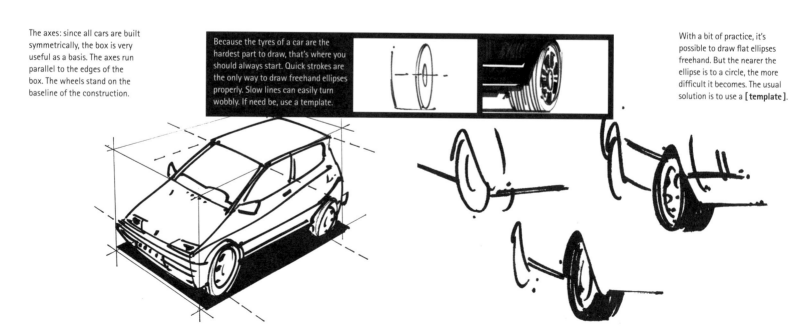

All objects are surrounded by spaces: narrow spaces within them and wide spaces outside them, which tell us where the objects are. It's often difficult to reproduce technical objects correctly or to show them from an interesting viewpoint. The unpractised among us tend to see cars as things with complicated shapes and lots of detail which they attempt to reproduce, only to discover that much of the resulting drawing is not quite right. Your task will seem much easier if you imagine that a car – like any other object – fits inside a box. This box has horizontal, vertical and parallel lines. Any kind of object imaginable can be cut out of this box, like a carving. What's important is that the perspective of the box is correct and has the rough proportions of the object to be drawn: in our case, a car.

The size of the tyres in relation to the car can say a lot. Broad tyres and a low-slung chassis make a car look faster – even when it's standing still.

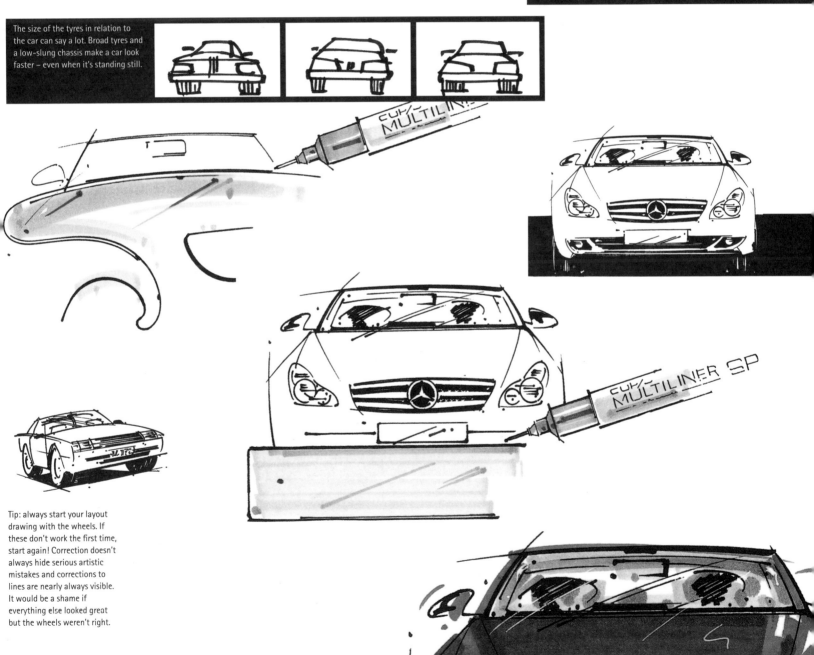

Tip: always start your layout drawing with the wheels. If these don't work the first time, start again! Correction doesn't always hide serious artistic mistakes and corrections to lines are nearly always visible. It would be a shame if everything else looked great but the wheels weren't right.

Extrem gut gebaut. Der Polo

We see the things we know. This holds true for the theme of cars too. A box, four wheels, headlights, windscreen and windows are the basic ingredients you need, so that even the roughest scribble can become a recognizable car.

If you're using scrap-file images as a source, all you need to copy is the construction lines. The lighting and colours can be changed in your own version.

The sun only shines when you say so...
and wherever you want

Keep shadows as contrasting as possible. If you're not sure, use a black marker. This always works and accentuates the technical aspect of the layout. Give heavy shadows sharp contours and keep them flat, drawing them with rapid lines.

62

Basically, cars are simple boxes with four wheels. To make them look a little more sophisticated, however, and to distinguish between the front, back and sides, contrasts of light and shade are useful. These differentiate the various sides of the car, give a more hi-tech look and breathe life into your layout. Whether large or small, quick shading sketches can be executed in a few lines and are important decision-making tools before you get started on more elaborate layouts.

Place heavy shadows so that they add depth and weight to the sketch. Colour can then be applied with the minimum risk of anything going wrong. Because our eyes fill in everything we know about an object, you can afford to leave out a lot of details in the layout. Just sketch the basic characteristics of the model in as few lines as possible. A point to note: if your line-drawn layout has the necessary oomph, then everything else is child's play and your cars will zoom into action!

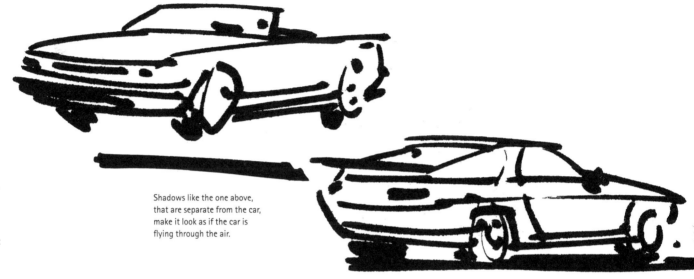

Cars shouldn't just look like rectangular boxes but should have a feel for form, technology and a sense of speed. If you're drawing a car, you should always try to show it from its best side.

Changing the lighting in a sketch can show how different variations have different effects. The right lighting can make an old banger into a real speed demon.

Shadows like the one above, that are separate from the car, make it look as if the car is flying through the air.

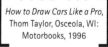

Small-format shading sketches can be done in a jiffy: make photocopies of your thumbnails, and then experiment by adding different lighting effects with a black marker. Use whichever visual effect looks the most exciting.

BOOK TIP

How to Draw Cars Like a Pro, Thom Taylor, Osceola, WI: Motorbooks, 1996

Careful: only apply large areas of black at the end, after the layout has been coloured. Doing it the other way around can cause smudging.

AUTO NEWS

Prototyp einer neuen Coupé-Generation: der Mercedes Vision CLS (li. u. re.). Oben: der legendäre Flügel-türer 300 SL und JLo mit dem CL 600.

Cars look sportier and have a sense of speed if some features are accentuated or exaggerated:
• Dynamic low angle
• Car placed on a diagonal in the picture
• Car cutting through the picture frame
• Wide tyres
• Wheels turned
• Low body
• Tyres set slightly above the ground or shadows
• Blurred background
• **[Speedlines]**
• Heavy shadows along the ground
• Strong contrast of light and dark in the windows
How many of these features you choose to use will, of course, depend on the idea you're trying to get across.

Ready to roll!

Three typical work stages: the original source image on a sheet of acetate, the line drawing and the finished full-colour version.

Remember: a car is basically a simple box. And simple boxes cast simple shadows, which need to match the lighting of the scene.

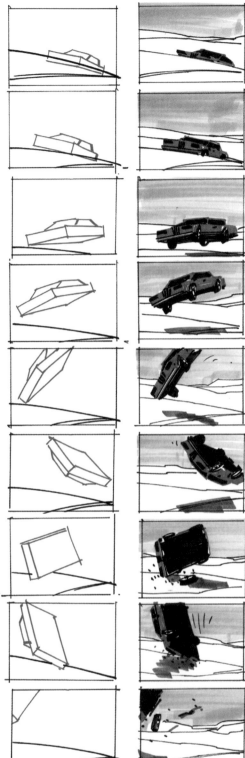

In this [**storyboard**] of a stunt scene, the path of movement is first mapped out by a simple box. This means that corrections can be quickly made and it's easy to move on to the next stage. The moving object (car) and static background (landscape) are drawn separately. This makes positioning the two layers in relation to one another easier and gives the storyboard its filmic quality. The second step is to add details that help to define the make of car. The last stage is to add colour – and already you can almost hear the squeal of skidding tyres and the crunch of metal on tarmac. Let's hope the driver's seatbelt was fastened....

Car windows are smooth and slightly curved and therefore reflective. As the windows of a car are at an angle of 90 degrees to one another, they each react differently to light. If you can see into the car on one side, it looks good if the windows on the other side are more intensely reflective. This emphasizes the characteristics of the materials used, and also adds depth by showing glimpses of the car interior. Keep the inside of a car dark. It adds to the illusion of depth.

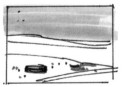

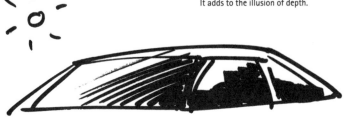

High performance:
from 0 to 400
in three seconds!

This sample layout by Thomas Heger shows how even a small-format layout can make a big impact. The original (right) was enlarged on a photocopier to 400 percent. Headlines and text can now be quickly added and the double-page ad is complete. The enormous enlargement has its own appeal with its quick lines and simple boldness of the motif. You can find some more tips on this technique on page 102.

Built for speed

Experiment to see which angles look the most dramatic and where the car should be positioned within the layout. A car that's poised to leave the page or the edge of the frame looks faster than a car that has a whole page to travel across.

If dark areas on the underside of the car coincide with the heavy shadows under it, then add sparkling highlights to the lower part of the car, to keep the two areas distinct. Alternatively, keep the shadows very dark and make the dark areas of the car a little lighter. Make sure that the shadows are not lighter than the underside of the car. The car shouldn't look like it's hovering in the air.

B 32

B 34

R 02

R 08

R 39

100

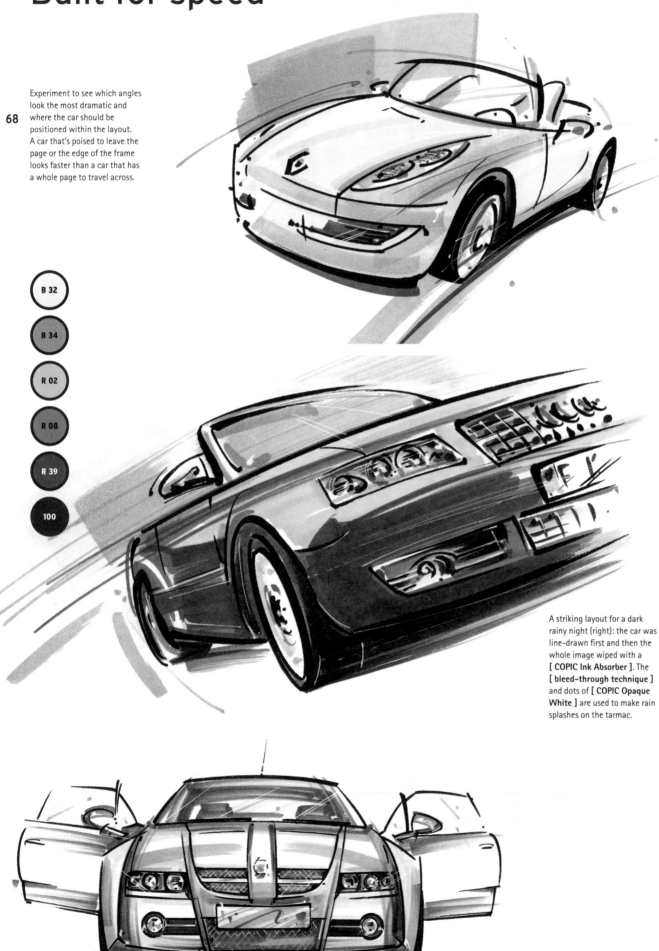

A striking layout for a dark rainy night (right): the car was line-drawn first and then the whole image wiped with a [COPIC Ink Absorber]. The [bleed–through technique] and dots of [COPIC Opaque White] are used to make rain splashes on the tarmac.

Sample drawings by Christian Felder, showing the three stages of a car layout:
Stage 1: even the variations in line pressure in the original drawing suggest speed.
Stage 2: bold dark areas are added, to add light and shade. The car is given more depth.

Stage 3: the colour spills over the black outlines. The hard shadow under the body of the car gives the car weight and keeps it anchored to the ground. Ready for a test drive!

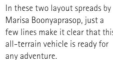

In these two layout spreads by Marisa Boonyaprasop, just a few lines make it clear that this all-terrain vehicle is ready for any adventure.

Stylish curves in only a few weeks! These samples from Wiesbaden students show how fast learning to draw layouts can be. Each car not only has its own look, but its own personal signature style.

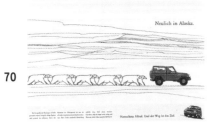

Sven Müller's storyboard is a dramatic, high-speed interpretation of the theme of a car chase.

This sporty Audi by Dirk Frömmer looks fast and powerful. This is emphasized by the low viewpoint, the broad tyres and the strong colour contrasts from light to dark.

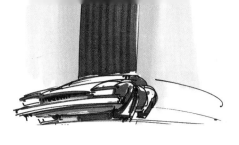

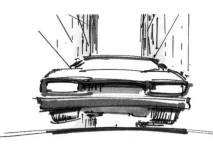

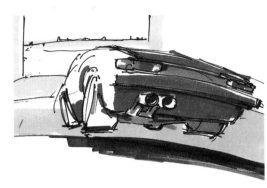

Rüdiger Schwarzkopf uses an exaggerated style and gives a speedy. cartoon-like feel to his red sports car.

On the road again...

[B O O K   T I P]
The Animators Workbook,
Tony White, New York:
Watson-Guptill, 1986

Only the construction lines are laid down in the preliminary drawing. All the other details are added at the next stage. In this profile view, horizontal speedlines add to the feeling of movement.

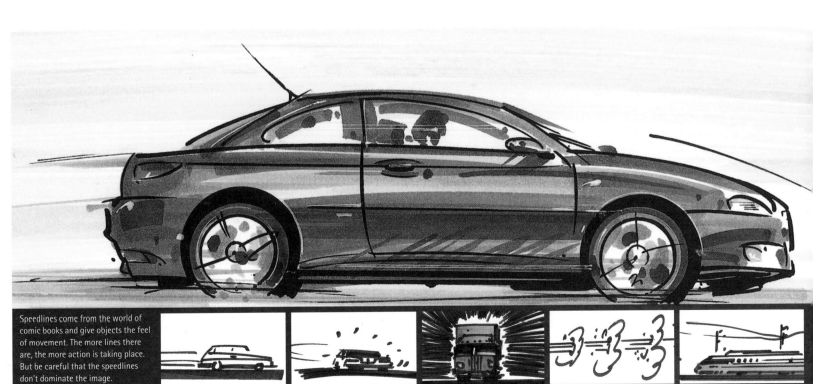

Speedlines come from the world of comic books and give objects the feel of movement. The more lines there are, the more action is taking place. But be careful that the speedlines don't dominate the image.

The rendering is a record of the current stage of a design process, usually of a technical product. It presents all the formal and functional innovations in an appealing way, usually from a striking viewpoint, dramatically lit. Product designers often work with special rendering paper, but sometimes use coloured paper instead.

These five car studies are by the young designer Björn Koop, and all executed in mixed media. He always begins by drawing the wheels. Then he adds the strong dark shadows that make the cars seem three-dimensional. The most striking feature is the lighting treatment that is applied to the basic line drawing. Details are then added that make the car an unmistakable example of its type. Finally, the whole image is coloured with [COPIC Markers]. Although he draws freehand, Koop also makes use of curves and templates to avoid the risk of errors.

Rendering car designs:
life in the fast lane

The low viewpoint of this image not only focuses attention on the car's bulky rear end, but also underlines the impression of power.

The dynamic treatment of lines exerts a sense of speed and makes the car look longer.

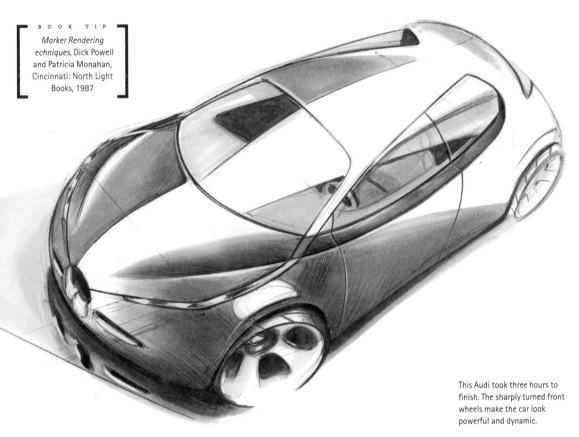

[BOOK TIP
Marker Rendering techniques, Dick Powell and Patricia Monahan, Cincinnati: North Light Books, 1987]

Björn Koop prefers to work in A3 format, which suits his personal style. Here are some tips for anyone who would like to explore this theme further:
• Keep experimenting with colours and search for new combinations.
• Always work from light to dark.
• To check the perspective, turn the image upside down or look at it in a mirror.
• Leave enough blank space around the body and wheels.
• Use pastels very sparingly: as little as possible, in fact.
• The wheels might not be the most important feature but they must look right.
• Include all the most important elements so that the car doesn't look as if it's missing something.
• Make sure everything is technically accurate enough to support your idea.

This Audi took three hours to finish. The sharply turned front wheels make the car look powerful and dynamic.

The car above is bisected by strong colour contrasts, which focus attention on the front half of the car. Fine hatching with a thin pen strengthens the shading.

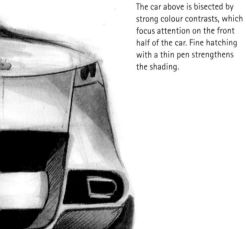

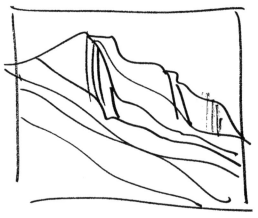

If you want to see the world, you've got to travel. Modes of transport may have changed but the characteristics of the landscape have remained much the same. So in layouts we use clear symbols and make only rough distinctions between flat, hilly or mountainous, lush green fields, dry desert or sparkling seaside. Scenery in a layout has the task of providing us with a description of the area, of creating an overall atmosphere and an illusion of depth.

The space of the landscape can become a stage for a wide variety of stories. A feeling of space and distance is most easily achieved with simple overlapping. Elements in the foreground are placed in front of those in the background, bringing life to the scene. Landscapes aren't dull and flat like planks of wood. Undulating ground, elevations, furrows and changing textures can bring even a flat field to life. Or simply imagine that the entire picture is a piece of rippling cloth.

The steep slopes of these mountain foothills are reminiscent of the flowing lines of a crumpled silk scarf.

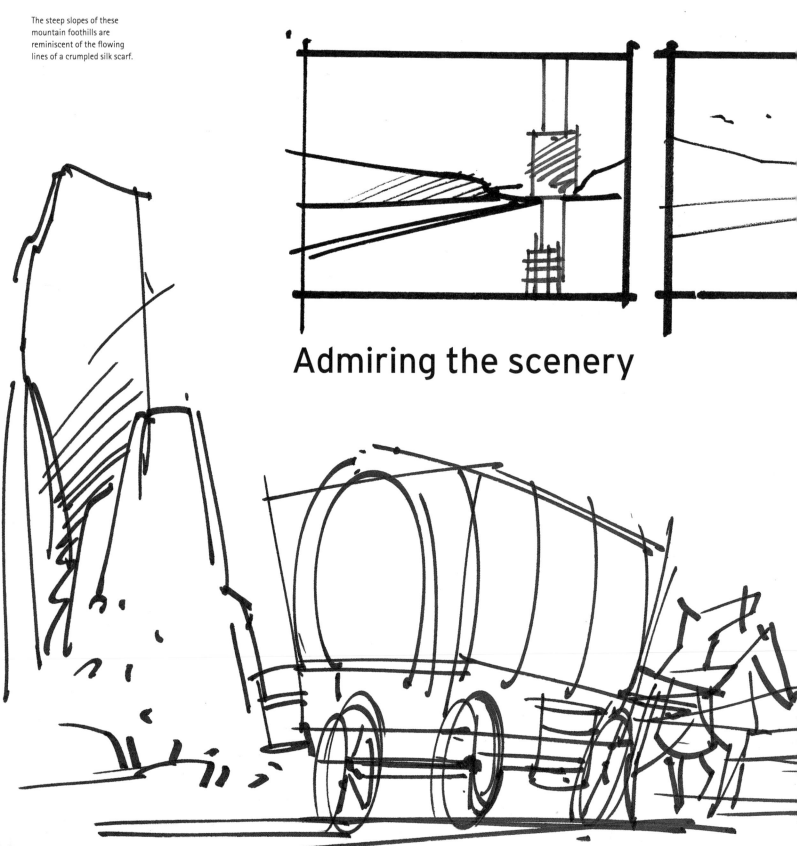

Admiring the scenery

The lines of the landscape should look organic, rather than technical, and should grow paler as they recede into the distance. Colour adds the final touch and completes the illusion. Never forget; quick, flowing lines and sweeping application of colour are always the key to success when visualizing ideas.

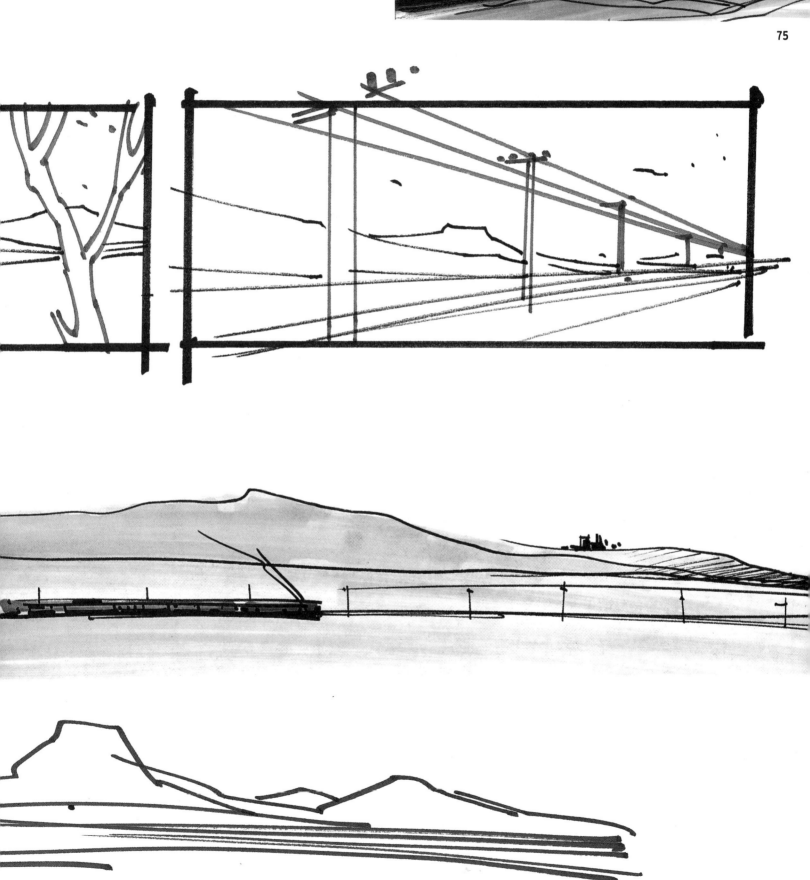

Landscapes play a part in almost all stories: think of them as accessories that help to build the right atmosphere. Landscapes must also remain muted when they're not playing a major role. Here's a short exercise that explains how to create idyllic mountain scenery, step by step.

1. Tear a piece of paper to leave a rough edge, and using this as a mask, draw in a pale blue sky with as few strokes as possible. This will create the white edges of the mountains. Incidentally, this is the simplest way to create an irregular mask, for clouds or sea foam for example.

A trip to the mountains
in six easy stages

2. Add a second layer of colour to the sky with the same pen, to give depth. The shaded sides of the mountains are also coloured in light blue. The mountain lake reflects the same colour.

B 32

G 21

B 34

Y 15

YG 17

3. Use a light, soft green between the lake and the mountains, breaking up the layer of colour.

4. Strengthen the mountain shadows with a stronger blue. This will add depth.

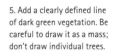

5. Add a clearly defined line of dark green vegetation. Be careful to draw it as a mass; don't draw individual trees.

6. The vegetation is softly reflected in the blue of the lake, drawing both elements together. Two yellow-green streaks in the foreground become a meadow, which fades back towards the lake.

B O O K   T I P
The Sketch In Color,
Robert S. Oliver, New York:
Van Nostrand Reinhold, 1983

Realistic landscapes have a sense of depth. It's good to use lines and bands because these take the viewer's gaze into the image and lead it into the distance.

A variation on the mountain motif, with the addition of a partial black outline. But if other features are going to be included in the foreground – for example a picnic – then it's best to omit any outlines from the landscape.

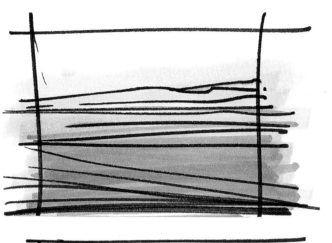

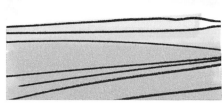

Colours are brighter on a summer's day than they are in dull weather. In the latter instance, the ink must be suitably subdued. Warm grey tones are very useful for this. For inspiration, take a look at the fantastic colour moods in Edward Hopper's paintings. His palette of bright and subtle colours is a joy to behold.

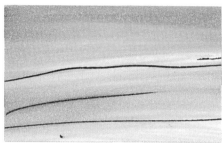

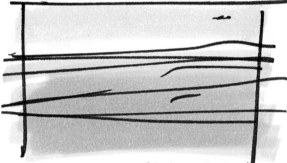

Start by drawing your landscape with no outlines at all. Apply colour in free strokes, adding the contours afterwards. You'll discover that this not only looks better but is much easier. Don't be nervous about applying colour; it's no problem if the different shades overlap and flow into one another.

Landscapes really come to life when colour is added. You don't have to use lots of different inks – just the right ones. There are so many natural shades that can be mixed from yellow green, lime green, olive, pale blue, putty, mustard, yellow and medium brown, and it's fun to experiment. Simply by applying the same colour several times you can create interesting nuances of the same basic ink. Try it out!

Colour knows no bounds. Always make your colour sketch larger than you need. Then decide on the section you want and cut it down with a scalpel to the size you need.

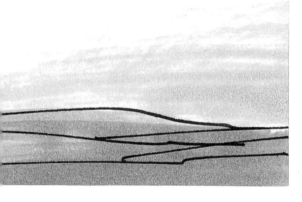

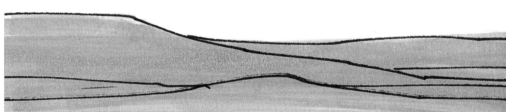

The choice of colour alone can turn rolling green fields into dry Sahara sand dunes.

Reflections on water and shining surfaces should always use paler colours. Only then can a clear distinction be made between the original and the reflections.

You decide what reflects, where, and how intensely. In this case, the three red banners are mirrored in pink in the lake.

Looks like we're in for stormy weather. Dark clouds set the colour mood of the layout.

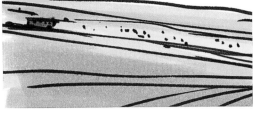

Before you get going on large-format layouts, small colour thumbnails using different light variations can be useful to help you to find the best viewpoint and lighting.

Is this a red shed on the edge of a cornfield or a bright red bus that has taken a wrong turning? We may never know!

[B O O K   T I P]
Edward Hopper: The Art and the Artist, Gail Levin, New York: Norton, 1980

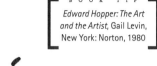

We all live under the same sky, but it doesn't always look that way

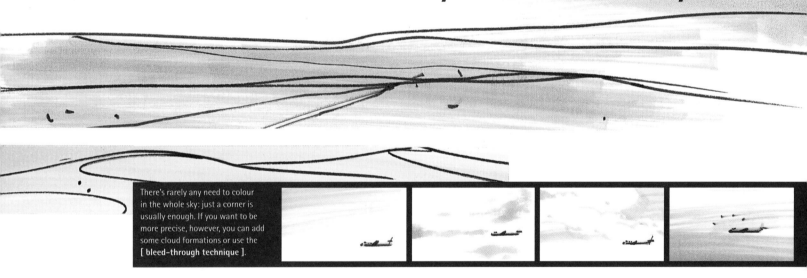

There's rarely any need to colour in the whole sky: just a corner is usually enough. If you want to be more precise, however, you can add some cloud formations or use the [bleed-through technique].

The sky is a major factor in creating a sense of space and atmosphere for the entire scene. Pale blue (B 32), a light, neutral blue, is always useful here. As with all other lighting effects for different times of day, the sky above a landscape should not be plastered in light blue. Sparing use of colour in the right places is enough.

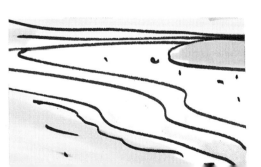

The waves lap gently on the sandy beach, but a splat of bright yellow suddenly turns them into a fried egg. What was the layout artist thinking about here, I wonder?

Look out – this tree is casting its shadow backwards.

Trees are actually easier to draw than most people think. If you need to draw particular types of tree, then concentrate on their typical proportions: narrow, wide, round, low, squat, conical.

Tree shapes can be easily drawn with outlines. Adding light and shade gives more depth.

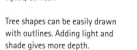

Can't see the wood for the trees?

Forget small details such as leaves, and focus instead on the overall shape of the tree top. Draw straight tree trunks with angled lines carried out in one quick stroke. This applies to both small- and large-format images. Trunks don't have to be chocolate brown; dark olive or even black looks much better.

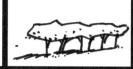   

Everything that grows in the wild has its own typical shape, structure and colour. Pay attention to these and build up your own repertoire of trees, bushes and other plants.

BOOK TIP
David Gentleman's London,
David Gentleman,
London: Weidenfeld and
Nicolson, 1982

No need to add lots of detail to large surface areas, especially when they are not central to the image. Whether it's blades of grass or the pile of a carpet, viewers only need a little information and their imaginations will do the rest.

Some trees, such as these palm trees, have an unusual structure. Avoid paying attention to details and concentrate on the essentials. Ink can be roughly applied to a line drawing and can be allowed to spill over the outlines (see overleaf).

The further away the object is from the observer, the more pared-down the drawing should be. A dark green blob on a stalk, placed on a pale ground, is enough to suggest a tree in a spring meadow.

Always draw tree tops as rough patches of colour. Start with a light tone and use a second tone to mark in shaded areas. In this way, you can plant whole forests in moments.

In this palm-filled paradise, it's important to distinguish between the green of the island and the blue of the lagoon. Therefore the bright blue of the sky is reduced to just a hint. The colours splash over the outlines, but still seem surprisingly precise.

A range of light and landscape studies from Wiesbaden students. It's the small format of these pictures, plus the lack of detail, that makes these colour sketches into mood studies. Mixed shades were created by trying out different colour combinations and applying more than one layer of ink. In the end, the eye thinks it can see more than is actually shown. Nothing can beat the power of imagination.

Winter landscapes are dominated by cold blue tones and the white of the paper. Shadows in snow should be drawn in light blue rather than black, which is too harsh.

The night sky is dark blue, so that objects that are darker still will stand out against the sky (see also pages 94–95).

Here's a sight for sore eyes! A beach holiday with plenty of sunshine and palm trees is something we can happily dream about for hours! Turquoise water splashes invitingly onto the hot, sandy beach, where holidaymakers are relaxing and enjoying themselves. In the foreground, two tanned bathing beauties go for a dip, and in the background, an oasis of palm trees offers cool shade. Behind the trees is a enormous hotel complex with a pastel facade. We think we can make out details, but the hotel is just a grid of horizontal and vertical lines that contrast with the organic lines of nature.

Sunshine, sea and waving palms

Colours in a landscape shouldn't fit exactly within outlines. They look much more lively when applied in bold strokes of colour, giving the illusion of wide-open spaces.

Water is life. Just a few lines are enough to transform a calm surface with splashes and waves.

Architecture: building a better layout

Architecture in large-format drawings requires a dynamic interplay of horizontal and vertical shapes. The Statue of Liberty looks out from her pedestal over a New York skyline that is made up of little more than a criss-crossing grid of lines. The textured sky over the city was created with [COPIC Wide] pens.

84

In a thumbnail, all you need is an interesting juxtaposition of lines, filled spaces and varied structures to create the illusion of a cityscape.

Buildings are an integral part of the landscape. When architectural constructions are arranged in an outside space, they acquire autonomy. Since we know that architecture is man-made, we are able to alter its different structures and rhythms. Using a mixture of key ingredients – horizontal, vertical and diagonal lines – and a choice of viewpoints, we can create any architectural object imaginable. First, we shall concentrate on producing line drawings of geometric objects and their structure, and defining their surface properties. The catalogue of materials given at the beginning of this book is extremely useful, as are [masks], which are invaluable when working quickly. It's also a good idea to study architectural drawings done by professionals. These embrace a wide range of different styles and useful approaches to the subject.

The fluctuating lines of Guido Ludes create balance from the complex architecture of cityscapes. Comic-book artist Chris Scheuer uses ink, cross-hatching and economy of line to chisel out contrasting architectural reliefs that leap out of the paper. Ivo Drpic creates sketches and coloured layouts executed entirely in freehand on tracing paper. And Ken Adam, the master of cinematic architecture, puts an emphasis on dramatic perspective with powerful, almost uncontrolled lines. These are just a few examples that might be useful in the search for a style of your own.

BOOK TIP
Everyday Matters:
A New York Diary,
Danny Gregory, New York:
Princeton Architectural
Press, 2003

Here's the same motif repeated four times, but using a different effect each time. The skyline below is very clearly constructed. The buildings are just rectangular pillars of differing widths and heights (like boxes on a supermarket shelf), and the facades are made from rows of repeated elements. Beside these well-defined structures, the architecture of the Sydney Opera House provides a striking contrast and appears to have been painted in.

Compared to the first sketch, the second image, at the bottom of the page, seems brighter and more airy, because the contrasts have been reduced. Curiously enough, the soft freehand lines do not clash with the strict technicality of the subject matter. Everything seems fleeting, reflecting the swift way it was put down on paper. A few strokes of light blue form the sky.

Think big, but keep it simple...

Unlike the first two sketches, this version uses ruled lines. Despite the hard edges, however, the lines fly across the paper and sometimes overshoot their mark, giving the picture the quick look of a sketch. The outlines are light and partially open, and the application of colour gives the buildings volume and substance.

Light and shade are sparingly used but are still plain to see. The drawing fades away into the background, giving the image a certain lightness. The subtle colours heighten this impression.

The layout at the bottom of this page is shown in a different light, as evening falls. The warm colours of the sky lie behind the buildings and provide a backdrop for the lighted windows of the skyscrapers. The water acts like a blue mirror, with the bright city lights mingling on its surface. The sky, the water and the buildings were all drawn separately then pasted up together. Everything looks much neater that way.

Every style of architecture has its own typical shapes: vertical and modern, medieval and provincial, or exotic and oriental. Look at the different types and try to capture them with just a few lines.

88

Here's a little exercise for you. Try drawing quick architectural sketches using only lines. Make sure that the lines close at the corners. Open corners give an unstable look.

If you're working with a ruler or mask, make sure that your drawing doesn't become too slow and accurate, or the final result will look dull. The lines should still be drawn quickly so as not to lose the sketchy feel. Crossed endpoints give your drawing the flourish of a freehand sketch, even when you're using a drawing aid.

Finally, add dark areas as shadows, to separate the buildings from each other. This makes your picture easier to interpret and creates a certain tension.

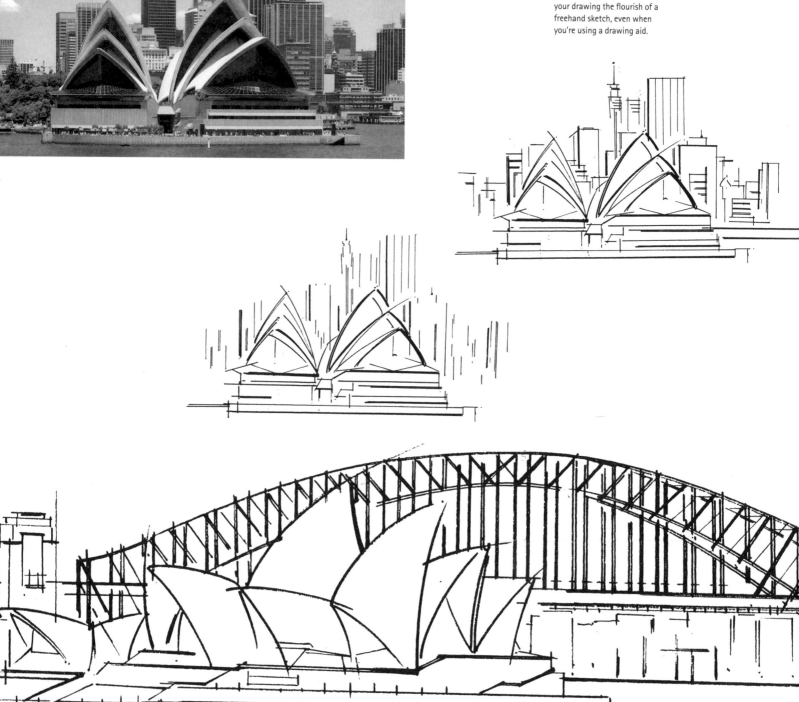

A [scrap file] can be useful when the motif is complex, the perspectives complicated or when the subject needs to be instantly recognizable. When copying source images onto tracing paper, only reproduce the main construction lines. All unnecessary details can be omitted. Always work methodically; trace all horizontal lines first using a mask or ruler, then turn the image around to find the best position to copy the verticals.

Overleaf, you will find a striking range of images that show the skyline of Frankfurt in different lights. Notice how detailed certain things look when seen from a distance. If you look more closely, you will see that there's not much there. Opaque white, small dots of colour and transfer lettering add flavour to the illustration.

The line drawing was only done once, then copied and coloured to represent different lighting conditions. The foreground and background were done separately, allowing the skies to be coloured in a single piece, using a [mask].

For an easy way to draw buildings at night, first do a normal line drawing. Then ink in dark areas where lights and reflective surfaces – for example windows – will go. Use a photocopier to produce a reversed-out image, and then ink in the colours you want in the white areas. Simple, isn't it?

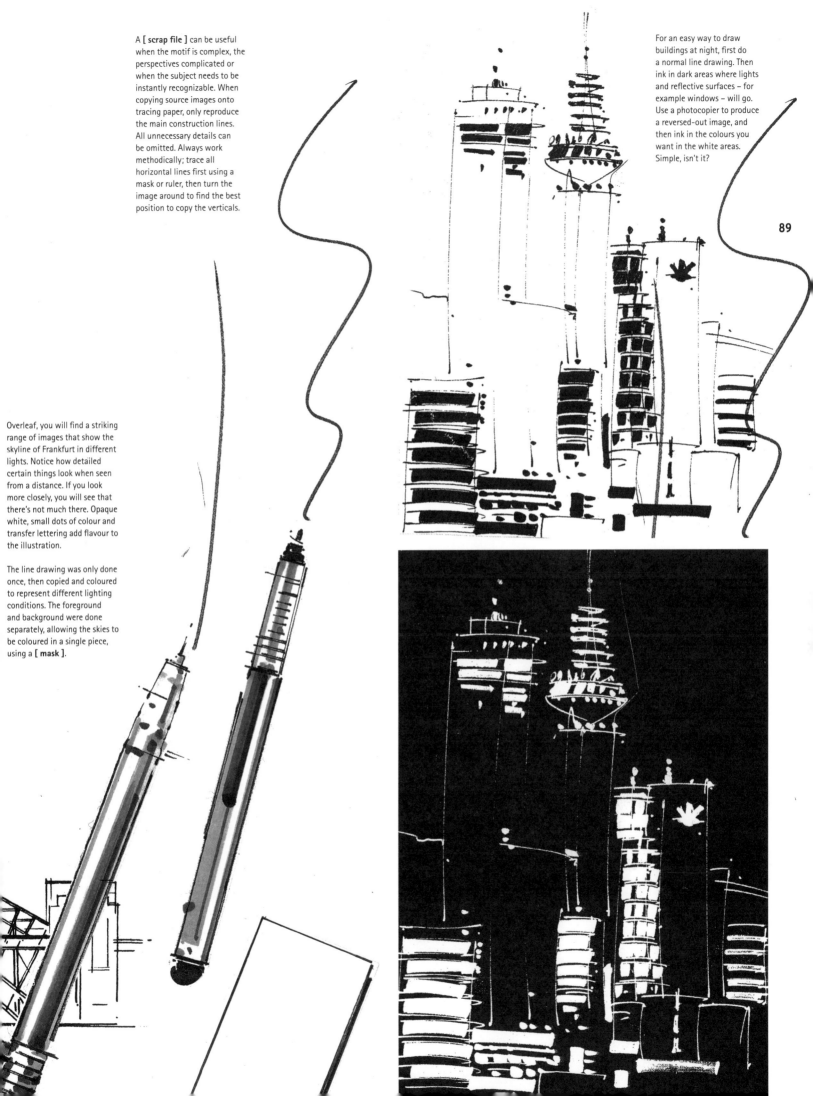

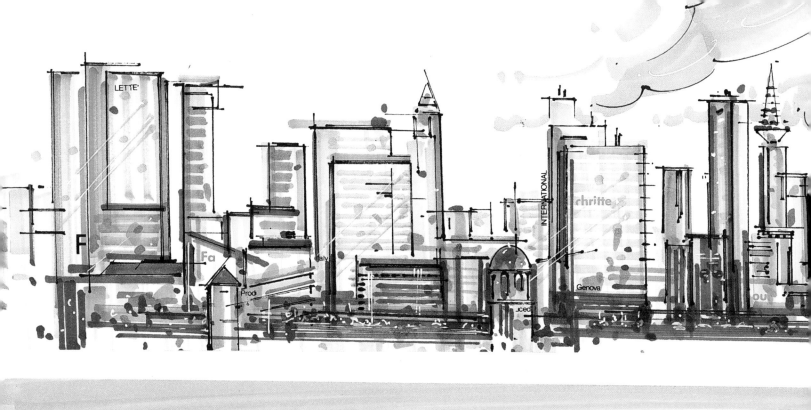

Admittedly, it's not easy to draw complex architectural designs from memory. It takes quite a bit of practice before you can create whole cityscapes. If you don't happen to have any suitable source images to hand, you can solve the problem another way. Below, we demonstrate step by step how to build up a whole district using only a simple street plan.

92

1. First, imagine a simple town plan. It has streets, crossroads and built areas. We now draw these on a flat surface, building up a plan we like.

2. The next stage is to tilt the map backwards until we find a perspective we like.

4. You may want to do a few small light and shade studies before pushing on to the next stage.

5. Then the facades of the individual buildings are given structure. Doors, rows of windows, canopies, balconies, shop windows – anything we think is important. Now all we need are the right colours and no one will know that just a short while ago, this business district was just a flat map.

In this airport layout, Susanne Schwalm shows how important it is to define individual buildings within a complex subject such as this.

A city scene by professional layout artist Thommy Mallmann. Architecture is defined by light and shade. The many light and dark splashes of colour create the illusion of a busy square.

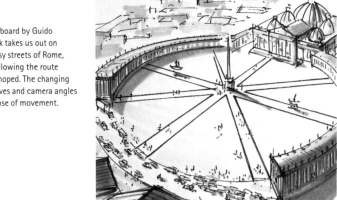

Every great architect starts with a simple plan

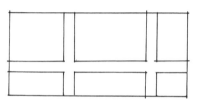

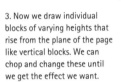

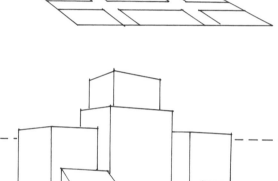

3. Now we draw individual blocks of varying heights that rise from the plane of the page like vertical blocks. We can chop and change these until we get the effect we want.

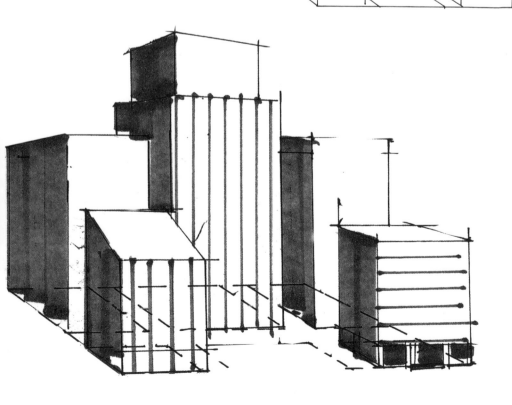

Looks like something from a thriller, doesn't it? The wedge of light on the ground dramatically points to the building as the source of light. The black blocks to the left and right of the picture intensify the feeling of being in a dark alleyway. Who's out there?

The greater the contrast between light and dark, the brighter an object looks. As shown on page 89, any sketch can be transformed into a night-time scene with the help of a photocopier. However, you might not always have access to a photocopier, in which case you can do it yourself.

First, do a plain line drawing with a ruler. This is important, as clearly defined areas of light and dark must be added later. All the light areas are roughly inked in, then black is inked over and around them. Always add the black last, or else it can smudge into the lighter areas.

Y 15

YG 03

B 32

B 14

R 08

RV 11

100

An exercise in lighting by Jörg Pelka (left). The brightly lit windows of this Berlin street invite you to take a night-time stroll. Away from the light, the buildings fade into the dark of night. Areas that lie between the artificial lights and the dusk appear in a greenish mixed light.

A bungalow in the park casts warm light onto the grass, flooding the lawn as far as the light reaches, then disappearing into the dark of the garden. The sultry summer night was created with the help of the [COPIC Airbrush System]. The graduated light in the sky adds depth.

The appeal of this architectural sketch lies in the fact that it was drawn on tracing paper. The colours look soft and cloudy, like watercolours. But watch out: when pale marker ink is applied over black, the black will smudge and look ugly. So when drawing on tracing paper, work from light to dark as far as possible, adding black areas last.

```
B O O K   T I P
Batman Animated,
Paul Dini and Chip Kidd,
New York: Harper, 1999
```

Modulating the light in the brightly coloured areas enlivens the facade of the building and creates depth.

Bright lights and city nights

An illuminating example (left): three different lighting treatments based on the same photocopied line drawing. They may all look highly detailed but in fact it's just the different structures, the quick lines and the high contrast that makes it seem so. Watch out – who is the dark figure lurking between the pillars on the left?

It's 1.32 a.m. and you're listening to the Late Show

Apply yellow as a base coat below other colours. This will increase brightness.

Whether you're drawing brightly lit office windows at night or the display on a radio, the process is the same for both layouts. Hopefully, someone will remember to put out this fire....

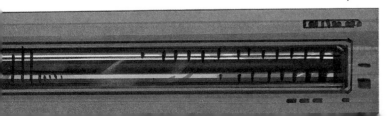

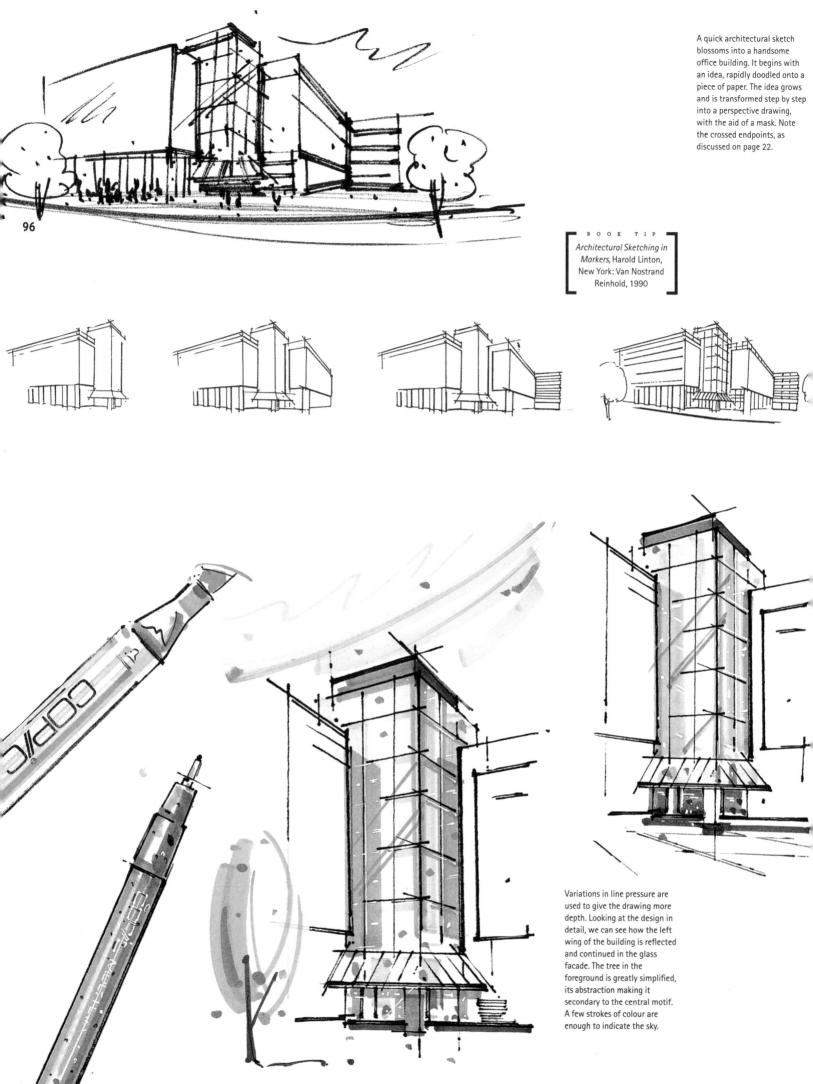

A quick architectural sketch blossoms into a handsome office building. It begins with an idea, rapidly doodled onto a piece of paper. The idea grows and is transformed step by step into a perspective drawing, with the aid of a mask. Note the crossed endpoints, as discussed on page 22.

[BOOK TIP
Architectural Sketching in Markers, Harold Linton, New York: Van Nostrand Reinhold, 1990]

Variations in line pressure are used to give the drawing more depth. Looking at the design in detail, we can see how the left wing of the building is reflected and continued in the glass facade. The tree in the foreground is greatly simplified, its abstraction making it secondary to the central motif. A few strokes of colour are enough to indicate the sky.

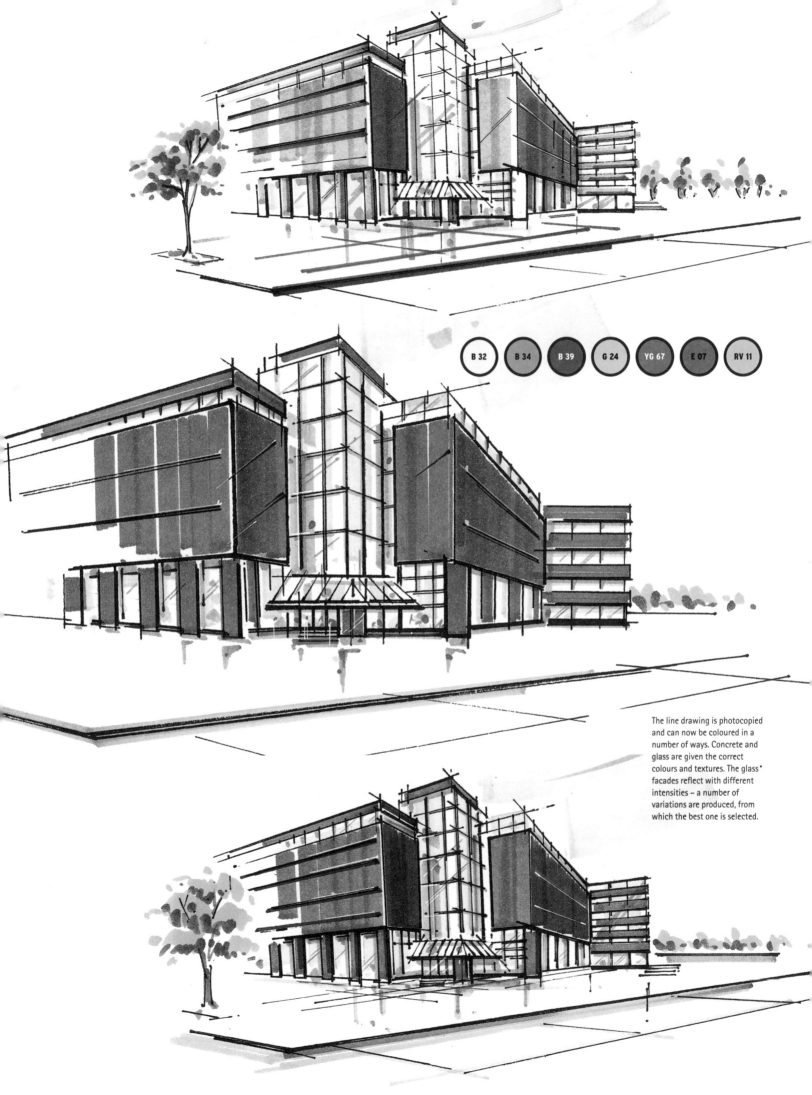

B 32 B 34 B 39 G 24 YG 67 E 07 RV 11

The line drawing is photocopied and can now be coloured in a number of ways. Concrete and glass are given the correct colours and textures. The glass* facades reflect with different intensities – a number of variations are produced, from which the best one is selected.

Look at things in a different light

Crowd scenes such as this one are drawn in a methodical way, just like anything else. Once the best viewpoint has been found, the room fills with life. All the figures are little more than repeated symbols: simple silhouettes, seemingly brought to life by contrasts of light and dark. Also striking is the contrast between the large figure in the foreground and the complex crowd motif in the background. Viewers feel as if they are standing in the gallery too, looking down on the hall below.

The aesthetics of different materials mean that professional layout artists have to carefully consider the best ways of presenting them. Thommy Mallmann has built up his own repertoire of materials and lighting and uses it time and again to effectively depict spaces and interiors. These examples from his portfolio show how important it is to pay careful attention to lighting. The perspectives, overlaps and changing temperatures of light in these high-contrast layouts are fascinating, captivating anyone who looks at them. Soft transitions are created with brush effects, while cold highlights are added with opaque ink. As flawless as these layouts look, if you examine them closely you will see that Thommy uses quick strokes of the pen and boldly executed lines. This is only possible when you know the effect you want to achieve and the way that different surfaces react to light.

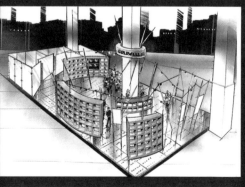

The specifics of location, viewpoint, lighting, action and casting were listed in the production plan and discussed with the photographer.

Design can be a pretty straightforward process when both the client and the artist agree on a concept for the project. The presentation of a brochure for a real estate firm required ideas for layouts that incorporated both text and illustrations. It was assumed that once the concept had been agreed upon, all the images would be replaced with photographs of specific locations, so this meant that the layout illustrations could be reduced to a minimum. The ideas were therefore sketched as thumbnails on transparent paper with a fineliner.

Each motif was then enlarged to A4 format, and light blue was used to suggest colour and depth. The enlargement makes the line drawing look dramatic by giving it depth. Although there is little detail, because the originals were so small, each image is clearly recognizable and shows everything that the final photograph should contain.

From small sketches to living large...

Wir können Ihnen

das Leben

ganz schön leicht machen.

In den weiteren Kapiteln werden begrifflich bewußt leichte Überschneidungen der Aussagen eingesetzt, um das interaktive Lesen zu ermöglichen. Die Textpassagen können bei jedem Thema unterschiedlich lang ausfallen, beginnen aber immer in gleicher Lesehöhe. Die Essenz der textlichen Aussagen ergibt sich für den Schnelleser durch optische Hervorhebungen innerhalb der Lesetexte...

Erfolgreich ist nur, wer den Standpunkt des anderen versteht.

Er hat lediglich die Aufgabe, zu zeigen, wie sich das spätere Textbild optisch präsentiert. Unter diesem Aspekt stellt sich CITY 7b beispielsweise als versierter Partner mit langjährigen Erfahrungen vor - besonders im Bereich der Altbausanierung. In den weiteren Kapiteln werden begrifflich bewußt

leichte Überschneidungen der Aussagen eingesetzt, um das interaktive Lesen (lesen, wo ich will, nicht wo ich muß) zu ermöglichen. Die Textpassagen können bei jedem Thema unterschiedlich lang ausfallen, beginnen aber immer in gleicher Lesehöhe. Die Essenz der textlichen Aussagen ergibt sich für den Schnelleser durch optische Hervorhebungen innerhalb der Lesetexte...

Er hat lediglich die Aufgabe, zu zeigen, wie sich das spätere Textbild optisch präsentiert. Unter diesem Aspekt stellt sich CITY 7b beispielsweise als versierter Partner mit langjährigen Erfahrungen vor - besonders im Bereich der Altbausanierung.

The photographer Norbert Guthier styled the final images, turning the rough sketches into scenes with his skilled eye for interior design. And the results look great, even if it's no easy matter to get a cat to stay on a balcony for long enough to get the right shot!

The thumbnails shown at their original size, before they were enlarged for the layout.

You've already seen on pages 66–67 how enlarging a doodle can save time and make your job much easier. Here, the little butler from a storyboard by Jürgen Schanz is enlarged to full-blown star status. Now colours can be filled in, or typography added, as shown in the examples below by Daniela Völlger and Peter Kohl.

The fastest way to make a
mountain out of a molehill...

IS YOUR DANDRUFF A HEADACHE?
TRY DERMACLEAN

Anyone with a photocopier can soon learn how quick and easy it is to turn thumbnail sketches into full-size spreads. If you scribble on a headline or slogan by hand, ideas can be quickly turned into entire campaigns, ready for presentation.

Night scenes are quick to do if you use the photocopying technique described on page 89. All the parts of the image that you want to be white should be filled in black first, before photocopying or scanning the image as a negative. The light areas can then be coloured in – and the candlelit dinner is ready.

W..SH WHITE.? ...IKES E"E.Y SIDE LOO.. BRIGHTE..

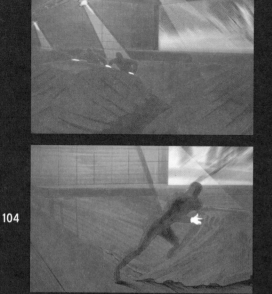

Work by three professional artists shows the key role that lighting plays in creating atmosphere. Hansi Helle's set design for a Daimler-Chrysler promotional event (left) uses cold blue light to create an air of mystery. Below, warm light fills his layouts for a different event in which guests move through various rooms decorated in the style of an ancient Egyptian temple.

Both examples show how important it is to decide on light sources and how warm or cold they are, and to coordinate the colours with the lighting within the layout.

An ancient temple and a duel by firelight

In this TV ad for Freixenet sparkling wine (left), a passionate visual and physical duel takes place by flickering firelight. In her layout for the CME & KHBB agency, Frauke Kärcher lets the warm light of the fireplace flood the pictures. The white of the paper is used for the highlights. The sides of objects turned away from the light sink into a strong darkness, which adds depth.

B O O K   T I P
Production Design,
Ken Adam,
exhibition catalogue,
Munich, 1994

A different Freixenet layout (above) by Thommy Mallmann strikes a far less mysterious tone: the glittering lights of a bar dominate the scene.

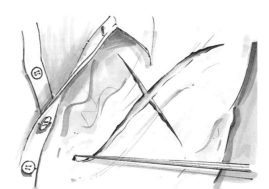

Now we've dealt with a number of themes and shown you a wide range of examples, we come to a subject that a lot of people find rather difficult: drawing people. Figure drawing requires knowledge of proportions, anatomy and posture – and that goes for layouts, too. But don't worry: using a catalogue of easily understood symbols, you can outline the basics. The best way to learn how to draw postures and poses in a few lines is to start off by drawing simple matchstick men. Head, body, hips, arms and legs are the main ingredients you need to create hundreds of striking stances and gestures. And if that isn't enough, you can use pictures torn out of catalogues and magazines or photos you've taken yourself to build up a scrap file of useful source material. Doodle as often as possible and wherever you are. Constant practice is the only way to learn useful short cuts. And be ready to draw spontaneously, whenever the opportunity arises. Just keep trying – all you need is a little patience.

106

[B O O K   T I P]

Markers Wet & Wild,
Charles Hayden, New York:
Watson-Guptill, 1993

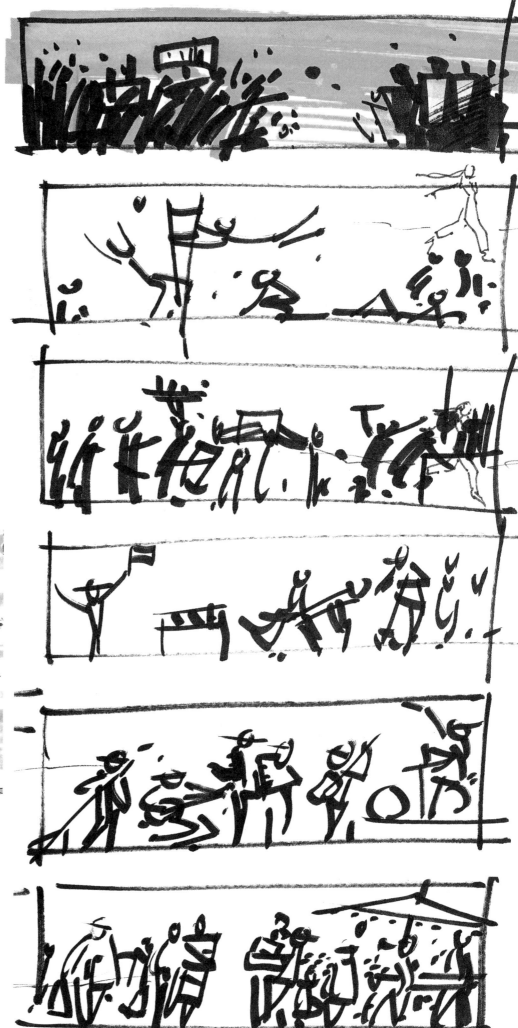

If you find it tricky to draw people from memory, buy a jointed wooden artist's doll. This can be arranged in any number of poses and positions – and never complains! Or look at some children's drawings: they never let complicated poses get in the way.

You can learn as much from watching Charlie Chaplin as any of the world's supermodels. Nonetheless, the exaggerated poses that fill fashion magazines can be very helpful when you're learning. Everyday poses with little expression are difficult to depict, because they lack strong features to give them character. If you're using figures in a scene, you need to find unambiguous poses.

Many situations can be doodled in a few lines. A political demonstration, an energetic tug of war or the hustle and bustle of a marketplace: compositions like these are powerful even without their details. The rhythm of the lines creates tension and contrast and gives an impression of the action in progress. Once you know how to set up scenes like this in a dramatic way, then you know you're ready to tackle other kinds of figure drawing.

Abstraction and minimalist depictions always require knowledge of the correlation between various parts of the body. Study figures and work out which parts of the body are tensed and which are relaxed. Observe the points at which the direction of the lines changes, where there are kinks and bends in the outlines, and why. Jot down figures without paying attention to clothes or other things; it's the posture that counts. The rest can be added later, like cloth draped over a shop-window dummy.

Doodle your figures step by step, on an increasingly large scale. Only minimal details are added, because these tend to be distracting. The enlargement of the woman and her dog demonstrates that even at this size, only a few details are necessary. The face is left blank, unless it's going to be a source of expression and information. The small curve becomes a hand because we know it can only be a hand. And the dog is recognizable because its proportions and relationship to the figure mean it can't be anything else.

Use a variety of drawing tools
when practising figures.
Different weights and qualities
of line have their own appeal.

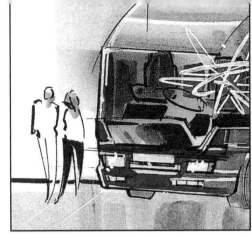

Even with this little exercise,
it's a good idea to try out
several rapid shading sketches.
In this way you can create a
sense of volume and depth
with minimal effort and
without letting detail get in
the way. This is important in
layouts where figures will
play only a minor role.

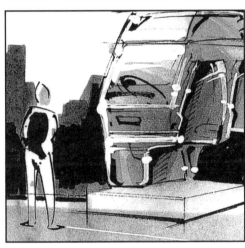

Bernhard Speh
(www.spehzies.de) has used
simplified figures to liven up
his illustration of an exhibition
stand. He has concentrated on
the typical poses of the visitors
– and little else. All other
details are omitted, as they
would be too distracting.

Less is more. The enlargement
of a thumbnail shows how little
you need to get the key points
across. A few lines capture the
calm, waiting stance of the
woman, her stylish look, jaunty
hat and small dog, who looks
as if he can see something that
we can't.

Torn-out images from newspapers, magazines and catalogues are the basic materials for building up your own scrap file. For a minimum outlay, you can combine different source images into a brand new illustration, as shown on the opposite page. When combining different images, you do need to check that the perspective you've chosen works for all of them.

For anyone who produces a lot of layouts, it's worth building up a [scrap file] (or 'morgue') of picture material. This will allow you to sort images by theme, add new ones when required, and generally save time. After all, there will always be some subjects that are difficult to draw from memory or too expensive to set up. For example, think about unusual perspectives, complicated technical or architectural subjects, or figures in complicated poses. A practical scrap file is well organized, manageable, and provides the right source images in just a few minutes.

If you can't find any suitable source images, grab your digital camera and capture the poses that you want. You can use this method to plan entire film sequences; it makes your job a lot easier when you have to produce a storyboard full of complicated motifs.

The right source material makes complicated images as easy as one, two, three...

The art director provided only this quick sketch as a basis for a Latin dance video. With the help of a digital camera, the most effective poses are quickly found and rendered as line drawings.

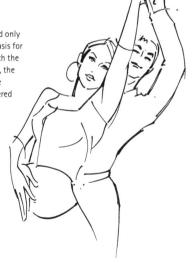

Just two or three basic images and a large format colour rendering provide enough material for an entire storyboard. Getting the right mood on paper is even easier if you have the right music to work with.

Montage: putting it all together

It's rare to find a source image that contains all your entire picture idea. And even then, it usually just contains the basic subject – not the attractive presentation and striking setting that you need. Different picture elements must also be made to match up properly. This is done using the [montage technique]. This means that elements from different source images are brought together and arranged into a single image. The individual pieces can be enlarged, reduced, improved and swapped around until the composition works. The whole thing can then be rendered as a single drawing and turned into a professional layout.

ÜBERGABE: 14.30 UHR
NA SUPER! DER DEAL IST GEPLATZT. ABER WIR HABEN DIE MILLIONEN IM KOFFER. ALSO NICHTS WIE WEG

To produce the finished drawing opposite, the following stages were required:
• Choose source images.
• Do line drawings.
• Check hairstyles
• Check proportions
• Combine the figures
• Arrange the scenery and any bystanders
• Trace the whole thing

Who would believe that these two stylish women out shopping have never seen each other before? It's not surprising when you realize that they both came from different magazines, and if it wasn't for the montage technique, they would never have met!

Practice and freehand doodling notwithstanding, there are always a few subjects that are much easier to draw from source images. For this example, we used a Christian Dior ad as a source; this chic lady, confidently striding along in her suit, was just what we were looking for. Her catwalk stride was particularly appealing. We copied her onto tracing paper, making sure to only duplicate the lines that were essential for posture and movement.

Leave out the shadows and all the other specifics from the ad. You only need the rough framework. Everything else should be redrawn to fit your own layout. Keep correcting and improving the traced image until you're happy with the result. Then move on to the next step.

Three colour variations, all using the same basic pose. The lighting is indicated by colour contrasts; areas of skin are only partially coloured and not completely filled in. Shadowed areas of skin have a light blue underlayer. For more about this, see page 124. When the colours were applied, some areas were deliberately left blank, to make use of the white of the paper. Pay careful attention to the feet in their elegant shoes; from a difficult viewpoint like this one, too many details can spoil the end result. Economical lines suggest just enough, but leave the rest to imagination.

Short cuts to sophistication

Suggest folds and creases in the fabric where the movement is greatest (legs and waist). Lines are relaxed and open. The illusion of movement is supported by partial gaps being left in the outlines and the effect of depth is enhanced by variations in line pressure. Lines are accentuated where depth is indicated, stressing the three-dimensionality.

The lines and dots of colour that surround the figure suggest energy and movement, rather like the visual language of cartoons.

[B O O K   T I P

Fashion Drawing in Vogue, William Packer, London: Thames & Hudson, 1983]

114

This step-by-step enlargement and reduction shows how details can be added and omitted. The clarity of posture and gesture remains unchanged, even in the smallest drawing.

The third variation struts across the page in a striking checked suit. The pattern is applied flat and undistorted, ignoring the movement of the fabric. This makes the picture less busy, yet expresses just as much. The fine white lines were overdrawn in opaque white ink.

Our model now has pastel tights and blonde hair. The strong light coming from the right washes out areas of colour, leaving white patches on the suit, the boxes and areas of skin.

What can you see?

If you're having trouble believing that a little can say a lot, here's a little test. This is an enlargement of the figure from the previous pages. Take a good look!

● The lines are very sparing, yet the changing pressure as they swell and fade adds depth.
● The principal areas of light and shade are implied by the line drawing, even before the colour is applied.
● The crossing lines or unjoined outlines give the motif its liveliness, particularly on the side where the light is coming from. To leave lines open in the sketch, you need to know what the finished layout is going to look like (colour, light and shade, environment). This must be considered right at the start.
● Details are suggested where they add structure to the motif (buttons, lips, glasses). Other details are omitted.
● The hair is treated as a flat surface, and lines are only added in the shaded areas to give depth.
● The face is made up of nothing more than the mouth and glasses. Anything else would make the area too dark and too crowded – and therefore illegible.

117

Faces can tell whole stories. However, we only want to say a few words about their structure here. Most people who tackle this tricky subject tend to overload the face with too much detail. Concentrate instead on the essentials, the shape of the face (long, round, oval or square), and outline this briefly. It's fine to allow the quick lines to fade away, because colour will be used for accentuation later on in the process.

Faces appear thinner and more structured when the cheekbone is accentuated by drawing a light line on the cheek.

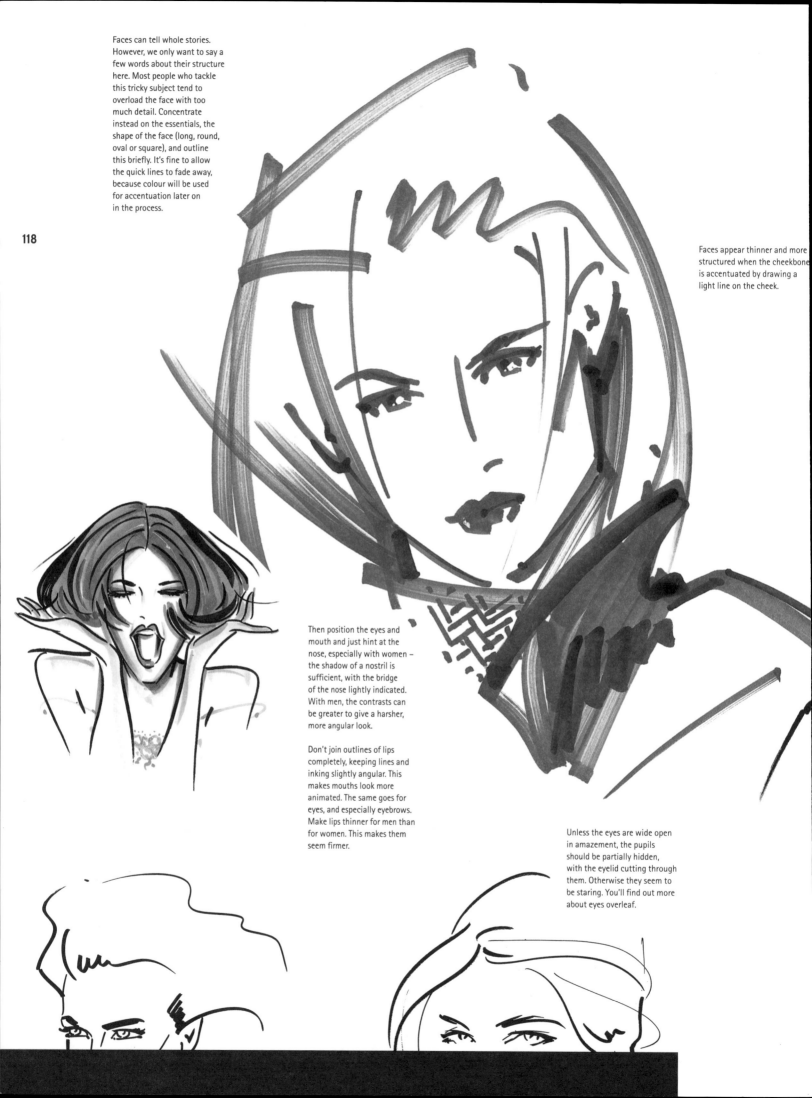

Then position the eyes and mouth and just hint at the nose, especially with women – the shadow of a nostril is sufficient, with the bridge of the nose lightly indicated. With men, the contrasts can be greater to give a harsher, more angular look.

Don't join outlines of lips completely, keeping lines and inking slightly angular. This makes mouths look more animated. The same goes for eyes, and especially eyebrows. Make lips thinner for men than for women. This makes them seem firmer.

Unless the eyes are wide open in amazement, the pupils should be partially hidden, with the eyelid cutting through them. Otherwise they seem to be staring. You'll find out more about eyes overleaf.

The face of your dreams

A small selection of hairstyles covers all the major variations: long and short hair, straight and wavy hair, and the difference between men's and women's haircuts. Today, of course, anything goes and it's often not obvious which haircut belongs to which sex.

Hair and hairstyles should be treated as volumes and drawn as outlines with minimum structure, especially on the side which is to appear heavier (the shaded side). This will make the hair look light and bright. Leave the transition from forehead to hairline open.

Keep the line of the neck straight and slightly exaggerate the length, but not as excessively as in fashion designs. If the neck and shoulders are visible, extend the neck straight into the upper body and don't let it curve around into the shoulders. The enlargement on the previous pages demonstrates what we mean by this.

In small-scale images, a suggestion of the eyes and mouth is sufficient.

120

B 34

B 39

YR 00

E 13

E 37

E 49

RV 11

RV 14

This Mona Lisa with her straight mid-length hair has a delicate complexion with a light blue tone in its shaded areas. Although the details of the drawing – done with the recognizable strokes of a [COPIC Sketch] – are very subtle, they will look great at typical layout scale. The background is filled in blue, using a [COPIC Wide].

Eyes are the mirrors of the soul, as the saying goes. We don't want to go into that much depth here, but it does go to show how crucial the eyes are in helping us to understand and interpret different moods and emotions. The most important thing with eyes is to learn the right way to capture the expression you want. Is your subject in a good mood or a bad mood? Is he or she angry, shocked or sad? Or about to burst out into laughter?

For most expressions, a few dots and lines are enough to show the viewer what you mean, but these have to be in the right places. Cartoonists are experts in this field and have mastered all the necessary shorthand.

Study the large line drawing below in detail. A couple of sweeping lines for the eyelids, a mere hint of pupil, the suggestion of lashes at the corners, and brows that are not exactly picture perfect. There's not a lot there, so the proportions and composition must be right. But don't ask for her phone number; this girl doesn't exist anywhere other than the world of imagination.

Observe faces, gestures and facial expressions around you. Make sketches of everything which seems striking or unusual. Cartoons and comic books can also provide valuable short cuts and bold examples.

Look into my eyes...

Pictures from magazines, newspapers or catalogues always come in useful. Copy the motifs onto tracing paper, simplifying them down to the bare essentials (less is more). Try out large and small versions, noticing how the number of details decreases as the picture gets smaller. When you've had some practice and feel confident, you can doodle when you're watching TV, or anywhere that there are people to watch. This forces you to draw quickly and gives you little time for thinking about it. Always remember: work quickly, even if it means that some of your lines don't look quite right.

BOOK TIP
Hand to Eye: Contemporary Illustration, Angus Hyland and Roanne Bell, London: Laurence King, 2003

When a person's facial and physical expression are important, make sure they can be easily interpreted. Think about what moods your figures need to convey and concentrate on these.

Eyes are alive and should behave as such. Let eyes react and pupils move. Eyelids and eyebrows bolster facial expressions and must be lively. Only sketch in eyelashes at the corners of the eyes, and keep them subtle.

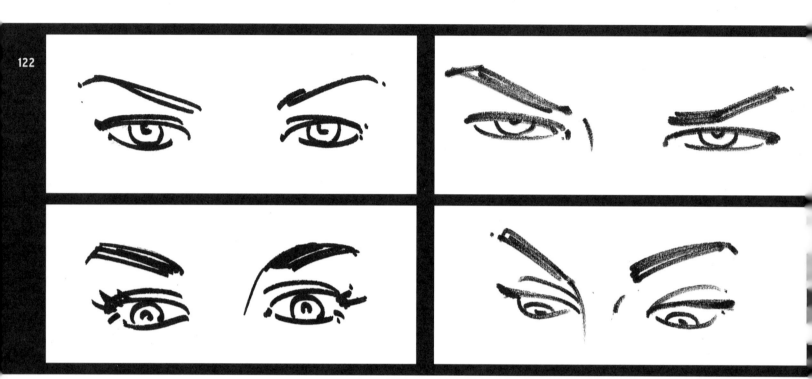

The eyes are the windows of the soul

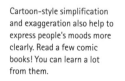

Cartoon-style simplification and exaggeration also help to express people's moods more clearly. Read a few comic books! You can learn a lot from them.

In small-format illustrations the line of the upper eyelid is the one that's important. The lower lid can be left out.

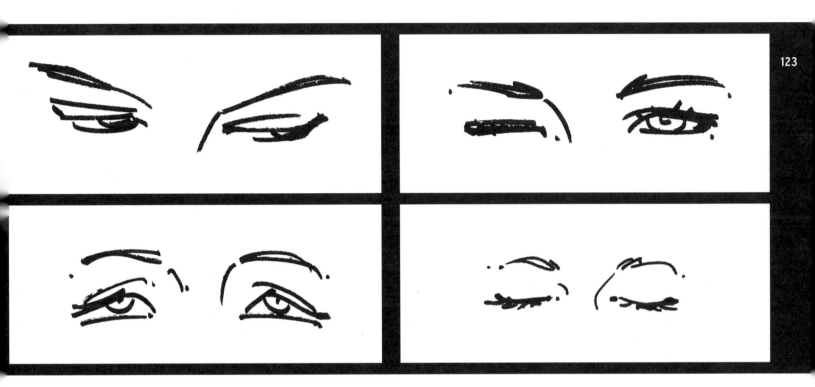

Eyebrows play a large part in facial expressions. If you look carefully you will see that the brows are not plucked and perfect but are put on paper with irregular lines. Brows can be different on each side; this brings life to your pictures and makes them appealing. Research has also shown that faces that are absolutely symmetrical look unnatural and masklike.

BOOK TIPS

Understanding Comics, Scott McCloud, New York: Harper, 1994

The Story of O, illustrated by Guido Crepax, New York: Grove Press, 1978

Ladies and gentlemen

More has probably been written about the differences between men and women than about any other topic, and naturally, this also includes the defining physical characteristics of both sexes. The scope of this book does not allow for a detailed discussion of this subject, so for that, we will refer you to the many good books that discuss the matter in greater depth.

Here we will concentrate on the many forms of shorthand used to draw layouts, using a male and a female 'model' as illustrations. The comparisons show what the characteristic traits of each sex are and how these small but important differences between the sexes can be put down on paper. Ladies first....

The blonde hair of this woman is drawn as a volume using only a few lines. The rather bright yellow is modulated by a darker shade and underlaid in blue in some areas of shadow. Blue is also used for the shadows on the skin. Most of the face has been left white, signalling where the light is coming from. Contours are soft, the lips full, the nose merely hinted at. The straight lines where the neck joins the body and the lines on the cheeks suggest slimness and give our model a fashionable elegance.

Whether you're drawing faces, hands, legs or bodies: never completely fill skin areas with ink. This makes them look ungainly and wooden.

Skin tones must be matched, using different combinations for different complexions. Skin colour for women is usually lighter and subtler than for men. Professional layout artists use blue to create shadows on warm skin colours, a technique used by the old masters. Why not try the same thing?

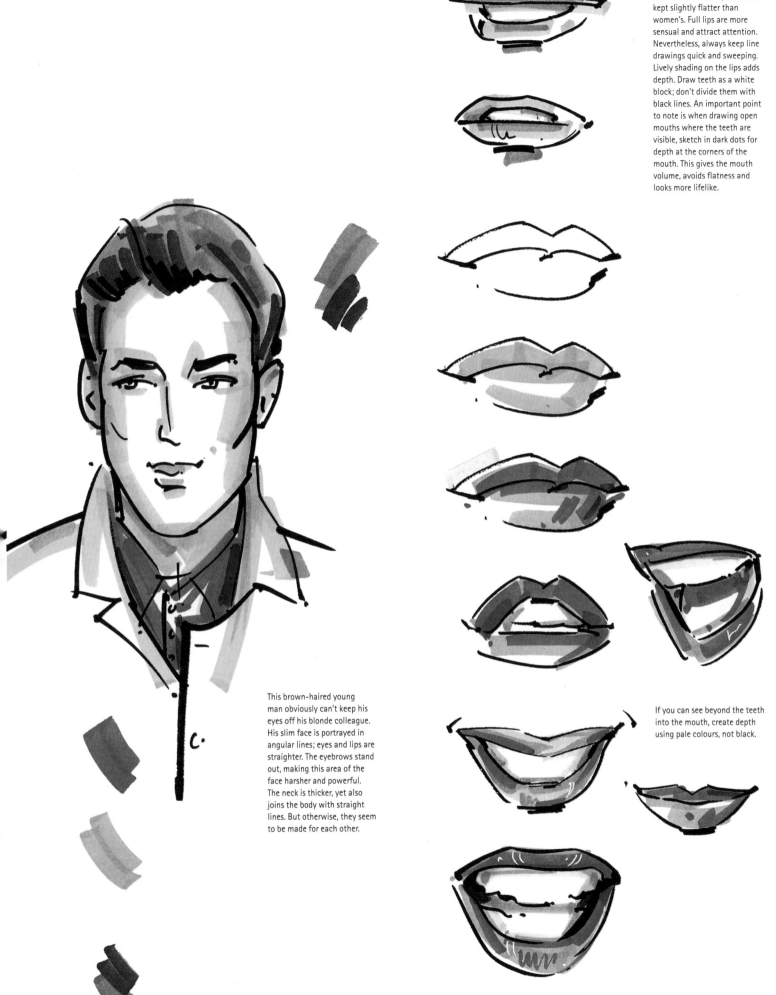

Mouths and lips emphasize the overall expression and bring a face to life. Men's lips are best kept slightly flatter than women's. Full lips are more sensual and attract attention. Nevertheless, always keep line drawings quick and sweeping. Lively shading on the lips adds depth. Draw teeth as a white block; don't divide them with black lines. An important point to note is when drawing open mouths where the teeth are visible, sketch in dark dots for depth at the corners of the mouth. This gives the mouth volume, avoids flatness and looks more lifelike.

This brown-haired young man obviously can't keep his eyes off his blonde colleague. His slim face is portrayed in angular lines; eyes and lips are straighter. The eyebrows stand out, making this area of the face harsher and powerful. The neck is thicker, yet also joins the body with straight lines. But otherwise, they seem to be made for each other.

If you can see beyond the teeth into the mouth, create depth using pale colours, not black.

This is another tricky subject and requires a knowledge of anatomy and movement. The only way to learn is to observe, analyse and simplify. Hands play an important role in any depiction of people in motion – they can grasp and move objects, point things out, be inviting or dismissive, or simply give emphasis to any message.

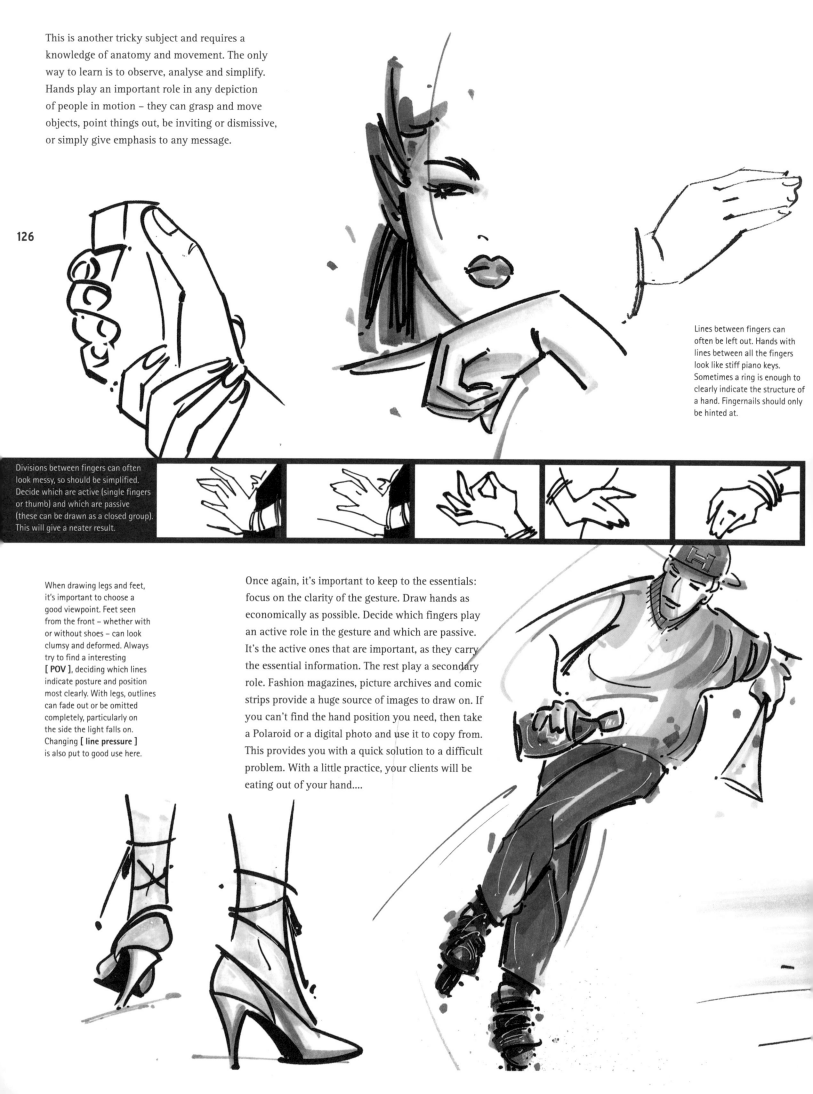

126

Lines between fingers can often be left out. Hands with lines between all the fingers look like stiff piano keys. Sometimes a ring is enough to clearly indicate the structure of a hand. Fingernails should only be hinted at.

Divisions between fingers can often look messy, so should be simplified. Decide which are active (single fingers or thumb) and which are passive (these can be drawn as a closed group). This will give a neater result.

When drawing legs and feet, it's important to choose a good viewpoint. Feet seen from the front – whether with or without shoes – can look clumsy and deformed. Always try to find a interesting [POV], deciding which lines indicate posture and position most clearly. With legs, outlines can fade out or be omitted completely, particularly on the side the light falls on. Changing [line pressure] is also put to good use here.

Once again, it's important to keep to the essentials: focus on the clarity of the gesture. Draw hands as economically as possible. Decide which fingers play an active role in the gesture and which are passive. It's the active ones that are important, as they carry the essential information. The rest play a secondary role. Fashion magazines, picture archives and comic strips provide a huge source of images to draw on. If you can't find the hand position you need, then take a Polaroid or a digital photo and use it to copy from. This provides you with a quick solution to a difficult problem. With a little practice, your clients will be eating out of your hand....

Men's and women's hands are different, particularly in their proportions. Female hands are slender and delicate, whereas male hands are broader and stronger.

Helpful hands and neat feet

The points at which feet come into contact with the ground should merge with whatever the ground is made of: grass, sand, snow, water and so on. This creates a link between the subject and its surroundings (see page 80 or 130).

Mixed media for tasty results

This TV ad for Barilla pasta featured German tennis star Steffi Graf professing her passion for pasta. The starting point for the ad was a set of thumbnails by the TBWA agency (top left), which outlined the basic scenes.

Nesrin Schlempp-Ülker then used soft, flowing lines, to keep the look of the subject soft against the dark background of the ad.

These early sketches show the difference between a drawing with changing line pressure, a brush-tip sketch and the classic marker layout.

Nesrin decided on a combination of brush-tip for the outlines and pastel chalk drawn over the top. The sole splash of colour, the yellow butterfly shape of the pasta, was added with markers. The delicious results show how important it is to choose the right tools for the job.

Musica.

Musica.

Musica.

Musica.

Musica.

Musica.

Musica.

Super: "Barilla. The choice of Italy."

This Barilla ad by the agency Young & Rubicam is an adaptation of an Italian production. The layouts for the 30-second ad were digitally produced. Music plays a big part in creating the right atmosphere for the story, in which Steffi Graf takes her friends to a restaurant and proves she really knows about pesto.

Figures that are raring to go

After all these rather sedate subjects, it's time to get up and go! Exaggerated movement is the essence of capturing sporty, vivacious figures, and requires quick lines and energetic use of colour. Experiment with different kinds of pen and line, and decide what works best for you. You'll find source material in abundance for this topic, but if you can't find what you need, you can draw doodles at your local playing field or sports centre, or from the TV. There are plenty of opportunities; it's up to you to make the most of them.

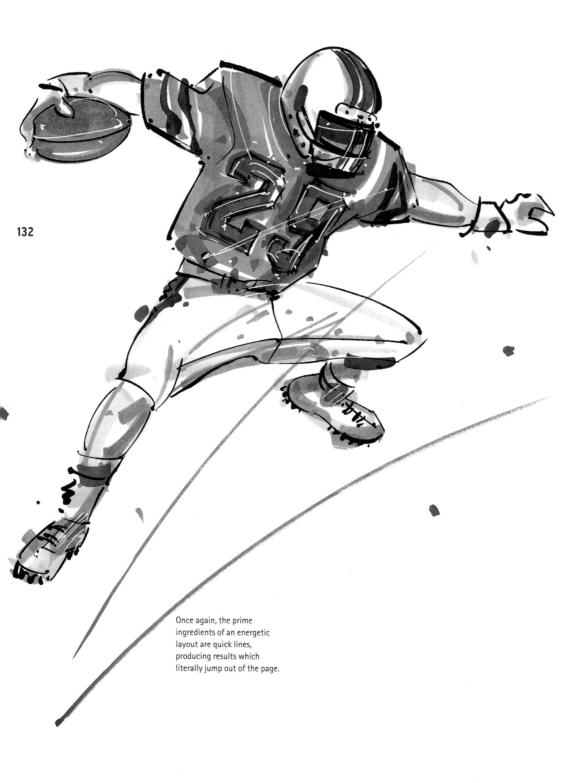

This American footballer (left) is just about to hurl the ball across the opposing team's line and is getting ready for a huge throw. The energy of the movement is enhanced by the exaggerated folds in his shirt, as well as the speedlines and small dots of colour, which almost look like a forcefield.

Once again, the prime ingredients of an energetic layout are quick lines, producing results which literally jump out of the page.

An unmistakable profile (left): the goalkeeper Oliver Kahn watches intently to see what the attacking striker will do next.

The player below takes a mighty jump and tries to throw the ball as far forwards as he can. His velocity is also suggested by dynamic speedlines, quick strokes and dramatic perspective. You can almost hear the noise of the crowd and the chants of the cheerleaders.

The exaggerated worm's-eye view makes these volleyball players look as if they're jumping even higher. A subtle airbrush effect is used to give the idea of depth.

Michael Weinerth's stylish layout (right) uses a very abstract figure combined with graphic elements to suggest movement. Speedlines also play an big part in the image.

Large areas of background appear boring and heavy when they are filled in with flat and repetitive colour. Nevertheless, sometimes large, coloured backgrounds are necessary, and this is where the [COPIC ink Absorber] comes in useful. Dipped in marker ink, it can turn any background into deep blue sea, cool surf or breaking waves in an instant. The sea spray in the windsurfer design can be done with [COPIC Opaque White], correction fluid, or by covering areas with masking fluid. The same goes for skies and other large areas that need a coloured fill.

The [COPIC Wide] saves lots of time and produces dynamic layouts. Although large filled areas of background always run the risk of overpowering the subject and not leaving any breathing space, coloured backgrounds done with this technique have a lively flow.

Two powerful strokes with a [COPIC Wide] and this swimmer is in her element. The colours underneath add shading and a sense of movement. The swimmer was simply masked with a roughly cut-out piece of paper before the blue water was added. A few highlights of the right colour, and the water really starts to move.

A tip when mounting: if the foreground motif is very light and is to be mounted on a dark background, stick it onto a second piece of layout paper before cutting it out. This makes the paper more opaque, preventing dark areas of background from showing through and spoiling the foreground motif.

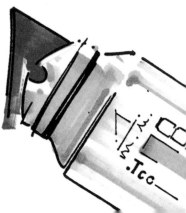

More examples of water in motion. The gushing drainpipe (far left) emphasizes the direction of the pouring water; the pelting rain (left) is highlighted by the strictly parallel lines of the falling raindrops; and the speedlines around the spraying hosepipe (below left) give a chaotic sense of movement.

Filling in the bigger picture... fast!

These two bathing beauties refuse to be impressed, and gaze impassively into the distance.

Before you begin work on a comprehensive layout, it's worth spending time thinking about the composition. These examples show how effective the right choices can be.

The downhill skiers opposite were drawn separately from the background, mounted and then surrounded with sweeping lines and realistically swirling flurries of snow. This gives a sense of speed and fun.

The thrilling descent of this snowboarder gets its liveliness from the use of the white paper. We can exploit the fact that paper is as white as snow by adding touches of colour for the background. Using the [COPIC Wide] or the [COPIC Ink Absorber], it's easy to add depth, transporting viewers to the snowy mountain slopes.

Exciting foregrounds need
backgrounds to match

Fashion in manga style

Manga comics are going through a huge boom in popularity at the moment, particularly among young people. A Japanese term, literally meaning 'random pictures', manga describes a typically Asian style of comic-book art. In Japan, manga artists are as famous as bestselling novelists. Mostly drawn in black and white, manga comics are popular with young and old alike. They often involve everyday characters (as opposed to superheroes) who get involved in all sorts of adventures, so the element of reader identification is high. Anyone interested in drawing manga can look at all the previous chapters in this book and use the ideas that they find there. However, the style and proportions of manga characters have a few notable features that make them unmistakably different from the figures in normal layouts. As we enter our fashion section, here's a brief guide to the differences when drawing manga-style figures.

BOOK TIPS

Manga Mania: How to Draw Japanese Comics, Christopher Hart, New York: Watson-Guptill, 2001

How to Draw Manga (series), Society for the Study of Manga Techniques, Tokyo: Japan Publications, 2001

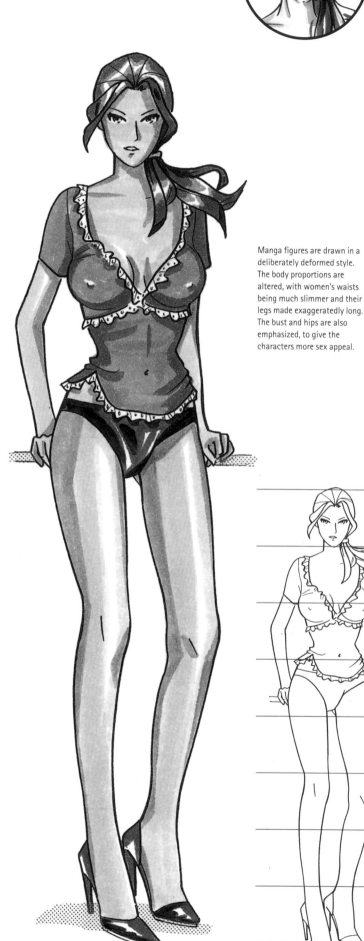

V 15

V 17

E 11

E 13

YR 14

E 37

E 49

B 32

B 34

B 39

G 02

Manga figures are drawn in a deliberately deformed style. The body proportions are altered, with women's waists being much slimmer and their legs made exaggeratedly long. The bust and hips are also emphasized, to give the characters more sex appeal.

The example on the right shows how the ultra-slim figure of the real-life model is made even slimmer in the manga version. The face is childlike, with its upper features much larger than life. This creates an even greater contrast with the curvy figure.

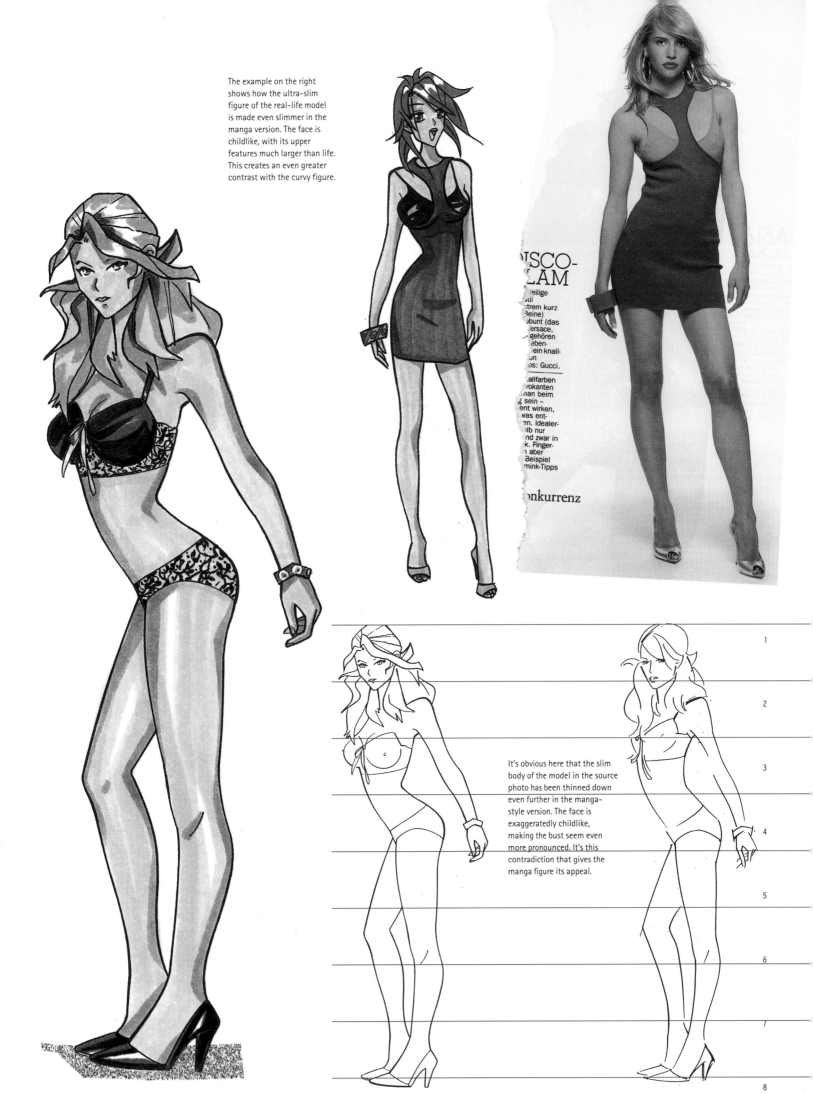

It's obvious here that the slim body of the model in the source photo has been thinned down even further in the manga-style version. The face is exaggeratedly childlike, making the bust seem even more pronounced. It's this contradiction that gives the manga figure its appeal.

One of the most striking features of the manga style is the unusual facial proportions. Faces are kept small but with a relatively low eyeline, giving a childlike look. Mouths are smaller, and chins weaker. The eyes and pupils are greatly enlarged, becoming the dominant part of the face. The childlike look is taken to extremes in both the character and the story. The huge eyes are mean to look cute and appealing and make the whole figure more expressive.

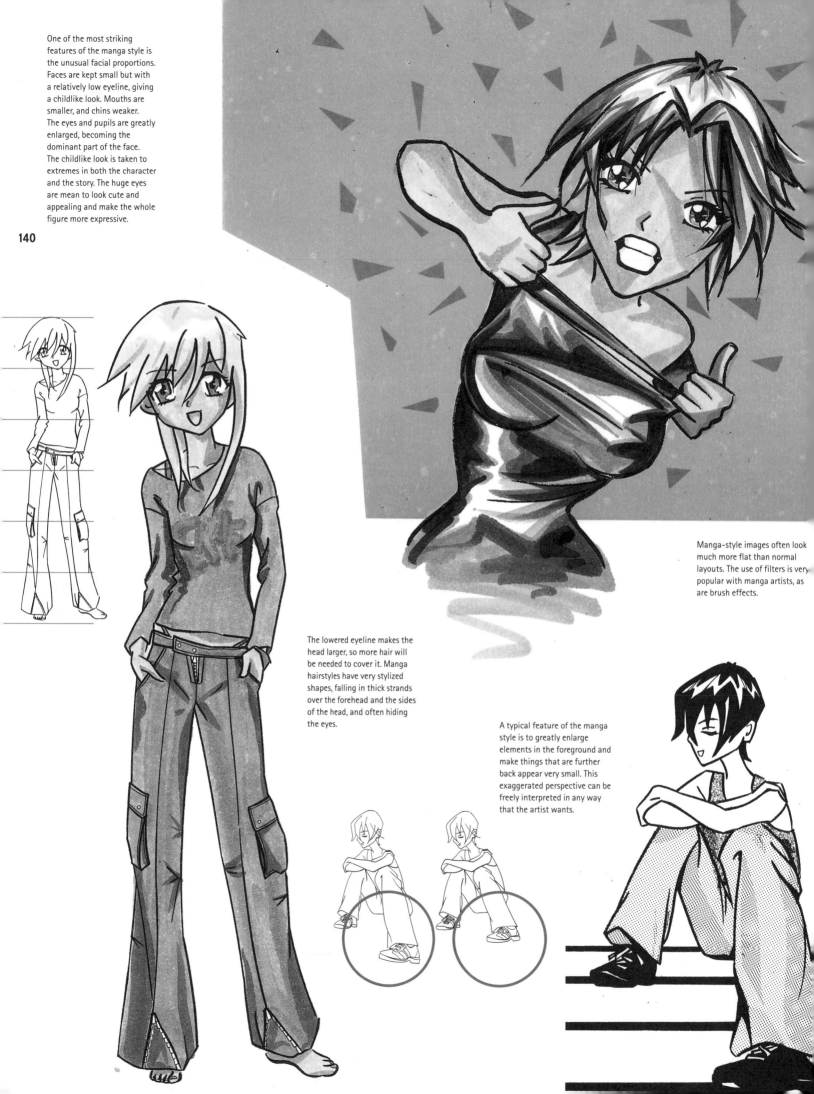

Manga-style images often look much more flat than normal layouts. The use of filters is very popular with manga artists, as are brush effects.

The lowered eyeline makes the head larger, so more hair will be needed to cover it. Manga hairstyles have very stylized shapes, falling in thick strands over the forehead and the sides of the head, and often hiding the eyes.

A typical feature of the manga style is to greatly enlarge elements in the foreground and make things that are further back appear very small. This exaggerated perspective can be freely interpreted in any way that the artist wants.

Many figures can be drawn entirely by computer. Using digital colouring, rasterizing and lighting effects, it's possible to build up entire picture sequences from scratch, putting manga artists at the forefront of digital art.

[B O O K   T I P]
The Japanese Experience: Inevitable, Margrit Brehm, Ostfildern: Hatje Cantz, 2003

141

Manga images can be anything that comes into an artist's imagination. Anything is allowed, as long as it is fun, fascinating and looks good – you could almost say that manga is the democratization of drawing.

When fashion is the subject matter, lines should be elegant and seductive. The appeal of the images relies on the recognizability of the central aspects of the design, with trivial details being left out. The main features must be emphasized, the essentials highlighted. The large image opposite attracts attention with its graphic, sweeping lines, while the lady peeping through her veil cuts an alluring figure. Incidentally, the veil is nothing more than the netting from a bag of fruit, photocopied into the picture.

What fashion dreams are made of

BOOK TIPS

Fashion Illustration Now,
Laird Borrelli, London:
Thames & Hudson, 2000

Fashion Illustration Next,
Laird Borrelli, London:
Thames & Hudson, 2003

On the next few pages we're not going to tackle the subject of fashion design as such, but deal with how fashion can be presented in a layout. It's important to make this distinction. Fashion designers emphasis different features and make use of their own individual styles and techniques (collages, mixed media, different supports, exaggerated proportions). Those wanting to explore this particular field need to be good at drawing people, learn the language of the world of fashion and study the trademark styles of the great names in the field.

We're just going to concentrate on one particular area, which shows how fashion models and fabrics can be rendered: from quick, rough sketches to what seem to be exact depictions. There are some things that fashion designs and fashion layouts do have in common, however: a love of strong poses, an emphasis on fabric and form, and a desire to fire up viewers with an appetite for haute couture.

This lady in red looks chic and stylish. But look again, and you'll see that everything is quickly drawn. The face is a bare outline with eyes and mouth, the hair is three or four carefully placed lines, and the skin tone is just a single stroke of colour. The red dress clings to her curves, and the fabric is simply suggested by a few carefully placed strokes.

The surfaces of different fabric react to light in different ways. Smooth fabrics are shiny, rough fabrics are covered with fibres or fluff. These can be depicted with little dots or lines. Nevertheless, keep fabric effects low-key and only use them as accents.

R 08
R 39
E 11
E 13
YR 04

Silk, towelling, wool?

Shiny

The model on the left illustrates how many different patterns of textile can be depicted with relatively little effort. The forehead, neck and torso are left open and suggest light. The face is drawn in just a few lines, and the hand is merely hinted at. The outfit is made up of flowing lines, and the legs disappear out of the bottom of the frame.

Left: patterns on fabric are always drawn clearly and without distortion. This gives the layout a less cluttered look. However, the fabric still seems to mould itself around the curves of the model. The skin is mostly left white with just one stroke of colour.

A fluffy bathrobe (below) is done with the [**bleed–through technique**] and a thin outline added with a [**COPIC Sketch**].

[BOOK TIP

Illustrating Fashion, Kathryn McKelvey and Janine Munslow, Oxford: Blackwell Science, 1997]

145

A transparent shimmering silk effect (far right): The layout was done on transparent paper then the colours were sprayed with fixative to produce the spotted pattern.

The patterns on these elegant tops (left) were done using tone-on-tone colouring on transparent paper.

transparent, fleecy?

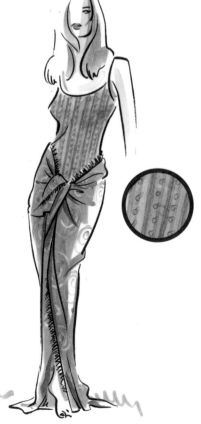

Pay particular attention to light, represented here by the white of the paper, which plays a leading role (right).

Fishnets from fruit bags!

Soft fabrics have folds, so lines must also be gentle and flowing – and, of course, always quick. The trick is to make shapes more defined in some areas and let them fade away in others. Partial black lines make the drawing clearer and add depth. Try out different kinds of line, depending on the size and style of the picture.

It's fun to see what you can make out of a good basic line drawing. Of course, you'll need suitable source material, which is essential for almost any figure-based layout. Perhaps it's a shame that drawing men's underwear doesn't allow for quite so many variations....

Fashionable colours vary according to the season and change rapidly, so would-be trendsetters need to keep up to date with the latest shades. The COPIC range with its 214 different colours means that you'll always have the newest trends close at hand.

The colouring and patterning of the fabric ignores the outlines and spills over them. This gives the design zest and further accentuates the lightness of the material.

Layouts can also let you find a use for things that would otherwise be thrown away. With a little imagination, some foil mesh or the netting from a bag of fruit can be used to add a touch of magic, by becoming fabric patterns or suggesting structure. Be creative!

On the left, a striking storyboard on the theme of a Lagerfeld fashion show. The frames skilfully record still details and scenes packed with movement, combining them in bright, fashionable colours to create the right atmosphere for the show. On the right, you don't need to go to Paris to reproduce the latest styles in layout form.

This pencil sketch shows which lines are crucial to the structure of the motif and which can be left out. It's essential that you learn to recognize this, especially when working from source images.

BOOK TIP
Fashion Design Drawing Course: Principles, Practice and Techniques: The Ultimate Guide for the Aspiring Fashion Artist, Caroline Tatham and Julian Seaman, London: Thames & Hudson, 2003

Our fashion section comes to a close with these three elegant catwalk models. All of them are reduced to the barest minimum of lines. The outlines are open, the faces are barely suggested, and the fabrics shroud the figures and look more like chance scribbles on the paper. The outfits and poses are the most important, while the bodies and skin are left to the viewer's imagination. Shoes and jewelry are reduced to coloured dots but are always correctly positioned.

Now that we've looked at drawing techniques and various common themes for layouts, it's time to steer our attention towards a very important area of graphic design: making storyboards.

Storyboards are sequences of still images used to plan a film or any sequence of events. Just think of all the TV ads, documentaries and training films, movies, cartoons and computer animations that are zapped out to millions of viewers each day. All of these begin life as storyboards, which determine how the final product, the film, will look. Storyboards rely on the major elements of pictorial narration, yet as a rule they differ from their historical predecessors, cartoons and comic strips, in that they don't usually include speech bubbles or panels. They're not there to be read, but to bridge the gap between completion of the script and the start of filming.

Storyboards suggest camera shots and give an impression of the atmosphere and scenery. Beside each frame is a description of the plot, information on camera angles and notes on what can be heard (dialogue, music, sound effects). Yet before even the first line is roughly doodled on paper, an idea must be produced, and it needs to be a good one.

Anyone that wants to make a film has a complicated job ahead of them, even with the incredible range of technical equipment that is available today. Time and cost-efficiency are dependent on finding the right combination of production method and design with the presentation of the product. So always bear the following points in mind:
• Any film project needs to be based on a good idea and a clear design.
• Films that present products are always only a part of an ad campaign and must be in keeping with and be integrated into the overall concept.
• The main points of the film should be noted down in a storyboard.
• A good screenplay builds up an exciting contrast of dialogue, commentary and moving images. Words should do more than simply repeat what the picture already says.
• A good film makes the best possible use of music and sound. These can provide background atmosphere, give emphasis or build up tension.
• If you want to make films, you need to become familiar with the methods and techniques of the trade in order to take practical considerations into account and make the right technical decisions.

Ads usually follow a set procedure. A team made up of an art director and copywriter put their heads together at the agency and try to find a good idea. They produce a brief description called a [treatment] and discuss it with the rest of the project team. The art director often doodles down his or her ideas on paper directly, detailing any important points next to the sketches.

Once the idea or sketched storyboard is 'approved' by the agency, it then goes to the client. Here, the procedure varies slightly: some merely present treatments (either with or without illustrations of the key scenes), others produce sketched storyboards. If this isn't done by the art director, then the agency may hire external layout artists or freelance illustrators. The amount of time and effort required depends on whether the clients trust the agency's creatives, and how much freedom they are given to visualize their project ideas.

In some instances, an [animatic] or animated storyboard is produced. The individual layout images are filmed, then edited together with a soundtrack to produce a proper short film. However, this takes time and costs money, of course.

The client, agency team and production company get together for a final discussion of the main points at the [PPM]. Then the serious and expensive part of the job begins.

Storyboards: putting it all together

storyboard templates are generally used when planning a film. The header contains details such as the agency, client, product, title and length of the film. The lefthand column is reserved for technical information (camera angles, lighting, editing) and the column on the right lists everything relating to sound (dialogue, music, sound effects), while the different shots are illustrated in the centre.

This book makes life easy for you by including a storyboard template on page 195. All you need to do is use a photocopier to enlarge or reduce it, and you'll be ready to design your own film sequences.

Good art and graphics shops also sell pre-printed storyboard templates, with windows for text and images cut out of A2 black card. All you have to do is affix your storyboard layout to the card backing and hey presto, it's finished! Making changes and corrections becomes quite a simple task. Sometimes, a presentation will involve an experimental format that uses an unusual arrangement of images or combines them with [moodboards]. Take a look at the following section of this book. Anything's possible, as long as it supports the initial idea, doesn't distract and clearly expresses what the finished film should be like.

B O O K   T I P S
Turnaround: A Memoir,
Milos Forman,
London: Faber, 1991

*Film Directing Shot by Shot:
Visualizing from Concept to
Screen*, Steven D. Katz, Studio
City, CA: Focal Press, 1991

151

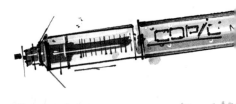
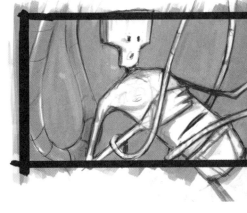

When the idea works, just a few lines can be enough to sketch out the plot for a client. As a warm-up for this topic, these simple storyboards from Wiesbaden students are all based on films, including *Titanic* and *Forrest Gump*. The aim was to keep words and visuals to a minimum but still get the plot of the film across.

Below are four totally different approaches to *Titanic*.

1

2

Ship goes on maiden voyage.
Boy in third class falls in love with girl from first class.
Her family don't approve.
Ship hits iceberg and sinks.
She lives, he doesn't.

3

4

Big stories
on a small scale

The thumbnails shown here, by Stefan Sperner, Joachim Brandenberg, Jürgen Schanz and Jasmin Siddiqui are all different, but all get the chosen story across. For the most part, they leave out the fancy details and concentrate on the basics of the plot. It's also interesting to take thumbnails like these to a photocopier and blow them up. If the lines are right, they should be able to withstand enlargement, as the picture on page 102 shows.

In this storyboard by Jasmin Siddiqui, it's amazing how recognizable the characters are, even on a small scale.

[B O O K T I P]
Exploring Storyboarding,
Wendy Tumminello, Clifton
Park, NY: Delmar, 2005

154

Any designer working on a storyboard needs to know which style of drawing is best suited to the subject matter. Are you selling a piece of technology or a beauty product? Is the plotline serious or funny? Should the characters be exaggerated? The art director and art buyer need to consider all the possible approaches before commissioning a freelancer to produce a piece of work. Then a layout artist is able to bring his or her own personal style and energy to the job. The examples below should make the difference clear.

A plain style: a small number of freehand lines are used to draw the subject in as straightforward a manner as possible. Speedlines strengthen the idea of movement. Things are drawn the way they are.

Action-packed: Steffen Winkler draws the same everyday objects with huge speedlines and exaggerated perspectives, giving the feel of a comic book.

Sci-fi style: Daniel Springer renders a sequence from *Star Wars* using clearly drawn objects with a technical treatment of lines, striking perspectives and strong light sources.

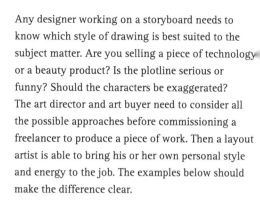

For a beauty product, Nesrin Schlempp-Ülker uses line and colour to draw a soft, feminine character, and uses light, sketchy outlines for the images.

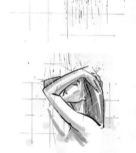

BOOK TIP
[*The Art of the Storyboard: Storyboarding for Film, TV, and Animation*, John Hart, Boston: Focal Press, 1999]

Every story needs a style of its own

Full of character: Silvia Püchner places a funny story against a more serious backdrop. Because the punchline needs to raise a laugh, a comic-book style is appropriate.

Cartoon style: Gregor Krisztian (left) uses a reduced number of lines to tell a story as succinctly as possibly, but he still leaves space for character and plot to shine through.

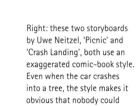

Right: these two storyboards by Uwe Neitzel, 'Picnic' and 'Crash Landing', both use an exaggerated comic-book style. Even when the car crashes into a tree, the style makes it obvious that nobody could have been killed.

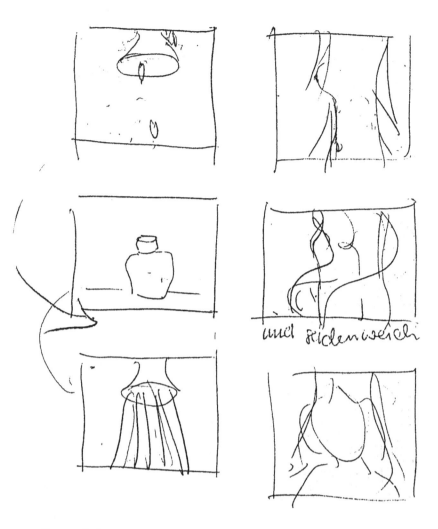

Day-to-day life at an ad agency involves not only the design of adverts, posters and promotions but also ads for TV and radio. These ads start life in the minds of advertising creatives, the art directors and copywriters. The art director starts by getting his or her basic ideas for a film down on paper. To do this, most agencies use their own templates with printed panels and space for comments. These include all important information on the client, the theme and the length of the ad.

Usually, rough thumbnails are enough to give the art director a feel for the storyline of the planned film and to discuss his or her ideas with other colleagues at the agency: the copywriters, creative director, producer and so on. Before the client ever sees the storyboard, the agency's in-house staff need to be convinced by it. If the idea survives the careful scrutiny of the team, it's okayed for further development. This cosmetics ad from the Lesch + Frey agency traces the typical path of an ad from the first scribble to the final presentation.

A day in the life of a storyboard

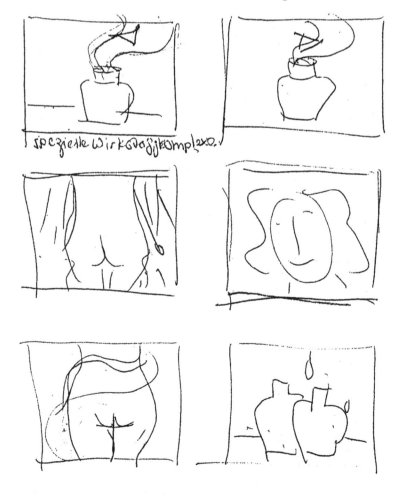

For this cosmetics ad, the layout artist was first given the art director's doodled storyboard by the agency and asked to work it up into a fully-fledged presentation.

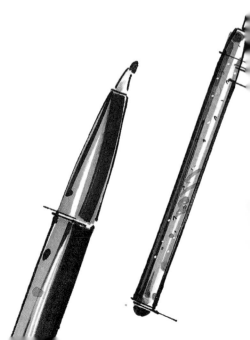

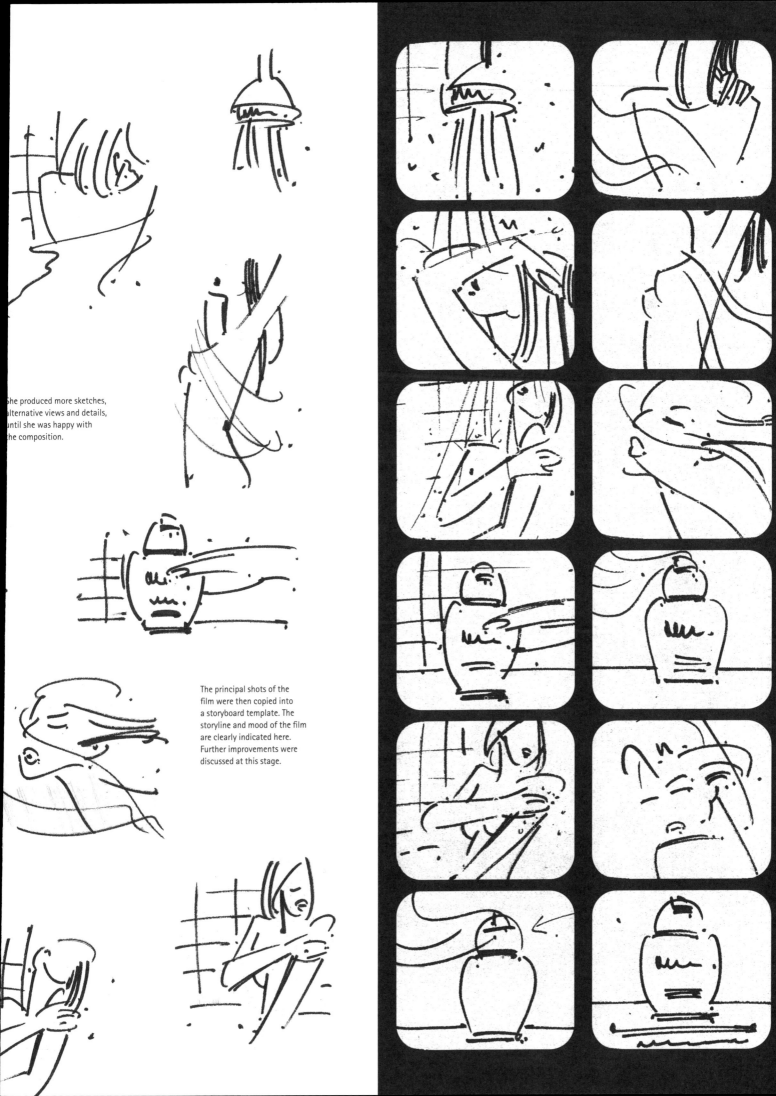

She produced more sketches,
alternative views and details,
until she was happy with
the composition.

The principal shots of the
film were then copied into
a storyboard template. The
storyline and mood of the film
are clearly indicated here.
Further improvements were
discussed at this stage.

Because the film was to be presented in the form of an [animatic], the individual pictures were enlarged to A4 size and coloured. Enlargement makes filming easier and allows the camera to zoom in and out of the image and create tracking shots.

Light, pastel colours underline the fact that this is a cosmetics ad and subtly contrast with the seductive lady in the shower. The entire board was filmed, music and voiceover were added and the project was successfully presented to the client.

The [COPIC Airbrush System] and [Ink Absorber] were used to create the smooth, even background of the pale green tiles. These tools make it easy to produce backgrounds and other large areas of colour. The dark tones of the skin and marked outlines make the few inking inaccuracies on the figure barely noticeable. Highlights in the water splashing out of the shower were added with [COPIC Opaque White] or a few dots of correction fluid.

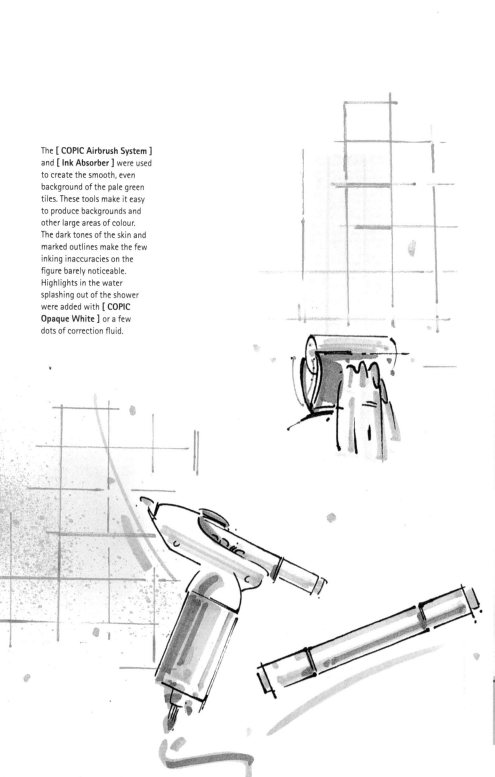

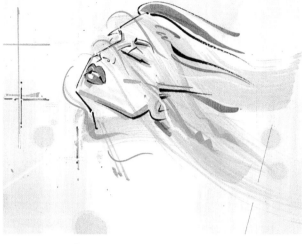

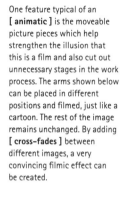

One feature typical of an [animatic] is the moveable picture pieces which help strengthen the illusion that this is a film and also cut out unnecessary stages in the work process. The arms shown below can be placed in different positions and filmed, just like a cartoon. The rest of the image remains unchanged. By adding [cross-fades] between different images, a very convincing filmic effect can be created.

159

A lot of time and money can be saved if you plan carefully before filming elaborate scenes and backgrounds. Our next example also shows how important it is to think things through before you begin.

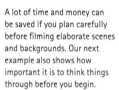

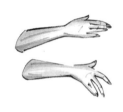

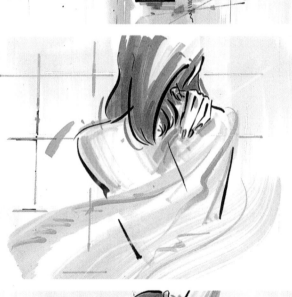

If you don't like commercially available [**storyboard templates**], then why not make your own? It doesn't take long to quickly create some panels by computer and add your own header before printing them out.

Whether a storyline looks better against a black or a white background depends – it's up to you to decide. If pale, pastel colours are used, your layout will probably stand out better with a black background.

② ③ ④

⑩ ⑪ ⑫

Silvia Wolff has chosen to present the storyboard below on traditional A2 panels.

The pictures have simply been stuck between the two layers of card with strips of tape. Changes to the images or text can be speedily carried out.

Halbtotale:
Ein Essen bei warmen Kerzenlicht mit ca. 6-8 Personen gemischten Alters. Der Tisch ist festlich gedeckt. Es herrscht eine angenehme, lebendige Atmosphäre, die Lichtstimmung soll die Leichtigkeit der Gesamtstimmung unterstützen.

Kamerafahrt über den Tisch:
Zu sehen ist der festlich gedeckte Tisch mit Servietten, Weingläsern und leichtem Essen.

Close-up:
Ein Gast prüft den Geschmack eines Weines. In der Hand hält er ein Weinglas.

Halbtotale:
Die Gastgeberin ist mit zwei anderen Gästen zu sehen.

Text Gastgeberin:
„Aufgepaßt, meine Lieben, jetzt kommt eine ganz besondere Überraschung."

Stefan Lochmann (www.si-design.de) chose to use his own format for his storyboard for Adidas Torsion shoes (Young & Rubicam). The horizontal ordering of the images accentuates the running motion in the film. Even at this early stage, the images capture the drama of the film and suggest unusual perspectives.

Halbtotale:
Ein Diener erscheint, in beiden Händen hält er ein gut gefülltes Tablett. Die Gäste staunen.

Close-up:
Frauen!...... .... das Produkt .... papier. Dahinter ist ein verführerischer Mund zu sehen.

Close-up:
Eine Frau genießt gerade mit sinnlichem Gesichtsausdruck unsere Praline.

Halbtotale.
Die Gäste greifen zu, unterhalten sich und genießen.

Planning a panoramic view

Interesting close-ups and
viewpoints can be singled out
and highlighted even at this
early stage. These will be
drawn separately later, as
individual scenes.

The following pages show how you can produce an impressive storyboard with the minimum of effort if it's planned in the right way. As a demonstration, we have whistled up a beach in a few quick lines. Like brainstorming, let yourself be driven by your ideas at this initial design phase, leaving out any superfluous details. Interesting features and sections of the image are marked and given careful thought, as this quick sketch forms the basis of everything that follows. It's not the details that are important but the dramatic structure of the image, the composition and any interesting close-ups that can be used in an [animatic].

The lead character is drawn in a few scribbled lines. The rest of the beach scene is brought to life by a number of relaxed, sun-soaked extras, whose outlines are sketchy but bold.

n the preliminary sketch, the central character also appears n a second position (above eft). We'll see why shortly.

B O O K   T I P
Storyboarding 101: A Crash Course in Professional Storyboarding, James O. Fraioli, Studio City, CA: Michael Wiese, 2000

Animatics: a story from a single layout

The tracking shot begins. Frame 1 sets the scene with a panoramic wide-angle shot of the colourful seashore.

Frame 2 covers a smaller area. The camera focuses on a group of holidaymakers relaxing in their deckchairs.

In frame 3 the camera zooms in even closer, enhancing the feeling of movement.

At the same level and distance as the previous shot, frame 4 pans along the beach to the right.

In the end, everything comes down to how good the idea is. So keep your layout as simple as possible, and don't spend too much time on it. In our example, we assume that the film will be presented in a way that's involving and easy to understand. With a few skilled strokes of the pen, the original doodle is now transformed into an impressive widescreen image. The summer atmosphere is created with splashes of bright colour. You can almost feel the heat and long to leap into the cool water. In the foreground, the pretty model reaches for a cold drink and waits for the camera to roll. Seven frames of differing sizes show the basic sequence of shots that will give the viewer the impression that these are moving pictures.

All frames are enlarged to the same size. This can be done by hand, on a photocopier or on film. The film can then have a soundtrack added, providing you with a presentation that's sure to impress your client. It's up to you to decide how much time and effort you need to invest in your layout in order to sell your idea.

Here's a closer look at the beach babe from our story. She has been drawn separately and is large enough to cover the smaller version of herself when she is placed against the beach background later.

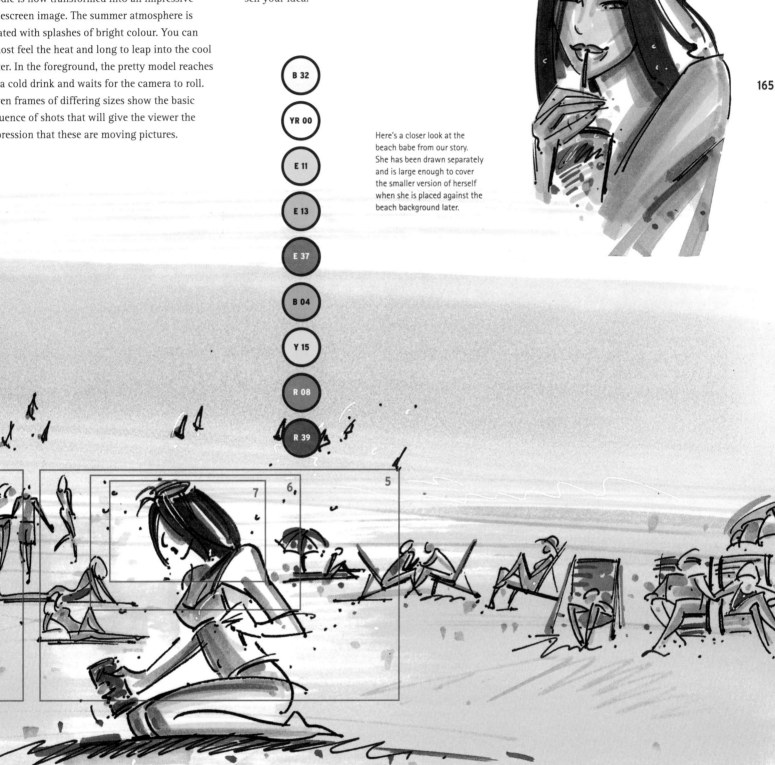

B 32

YR 00

E 11

E 13

E 37

B 04

Y 15

R 08

R 39

Frame 5 takes a medium shot of the star. We notice that the camera focuses on her.

In frame 6, the camera zooms in on the girl and stops in frame 7 with a close-up of her in profile.

BOOK TIP

Setting Up Your Shots: Great Camera Moves Every Filmmaker Should Know, Jeremy Vineyard, Studio City, CA: Michael Wiese Productions, 2000

Frames 1 to 3 show the camera
zooming in on the scene.

The camera pans horizontally
along the beach, homing in on
our heroine.

The camera zooms in again,
this time on the woman's face,
showing that she's the key
figure in the story.

.If you're happy with your basic layout
and want to try out some different
colour variations, photocopy the line
drawing and go over it with markers.
Make sure you use the right side of the
paper when you put it in the copier.

From still images to moving pictures

When the individual frames are shown in rapid succession, viewers will get the impression that the pictures are moving – in all senses of the word. Our imaginations tend to link the shots together and fill in any gaps, creating a running film in our minds. With effective detail shots, interesting changes of frame and exciting perspectives added, the same storyboard can be used to create many different moods: from dreamlike to documentary to thriller. Try your hand at directing your own version.

BOOK TIPS

Comics & Sequential Art,
Will Eisner,
Tamarac, FL: Poorhouse
Press, 1985

*Aladdin: The Making
of an Animated Film*,
John Culhane, New York:
Hyperion, 1992

The arrangement of the pictures in storyboard format on these two pages shows that the ordering of the frames can also enhance movement.

Cut to a close-up, showing the girl opening a fizzy drink. The camera follows the straw from the girl's hands to her mouth as she takes a sip.

The second version of the figure is now overlaid in position. The camera focuses on her face and zooms in on her eyes, which reflect the clear blue of the sea.

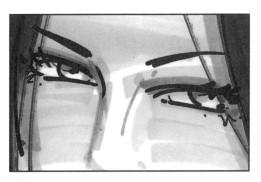

Let's assume that we don't want our beach babe to look as bold as this, and want her to be shyly closing her eyes instead.

Professional layout artists are very pragmatic. They know that a layout is just a means to an end and is unlikely to end up hanging on someone's wall. So layouts are produced as efficiently as possible: quickly, simply, yet saying what they need to. Corrections, alterations and amendments are, however, all part of the daily routine and usually have to be carried out very quickly. Professionals are also very inventive. Minor corrections or alterations normally involve reworking only small sections of the layout. The solution is often to simply stick the new version of the image over the old one. This can be done accurately and cleanly by cutting problem areas out of the layout and inlaying the correct ones in exactly the same place (see page 42). This prevents jagged, cut edges which look messy. The layout is then photocopied and no one is any the wiser. It's all quite simple.

Take the first drawing and place a strip of paper over the eyes, fixed to the page with sticky tape. The chosen area can now be changed in any way you like.

Use a scalpel to cut through both layers of paper at the same time. Then remove the original eyes and use [spray adhesive] to stick down the new ones, which will fit exactly into the slot. Finally, smooth down the edges with your fingernail. All finished!

Changes and corrections: quick, easy and invisible

A quick correction method. Motifs 1 and 2 were drawn separately, then correctly positioned and fixed down with tape. Then a scalpel was used to cut through both layers, so that motif 1 fits into the hole in motif 2.

Motifs of different sizes vary in their line quality and detail, but not in their speed. The smaller the motif, the fewer lines, details and colours there are. Keep the outlines open; it makes your doodles look lighter and more lively.

In a brochure presentation, the sticky tape that holds the pages together should not be visible. So fix the pages together first and then stick the layouts on top. Cut off any overhanging edges, and no one will notice any joins.

As soon as a pretty girl arrives on the beach, the boys swarm around her like flies. And it doesn't only happen on TV....

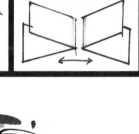

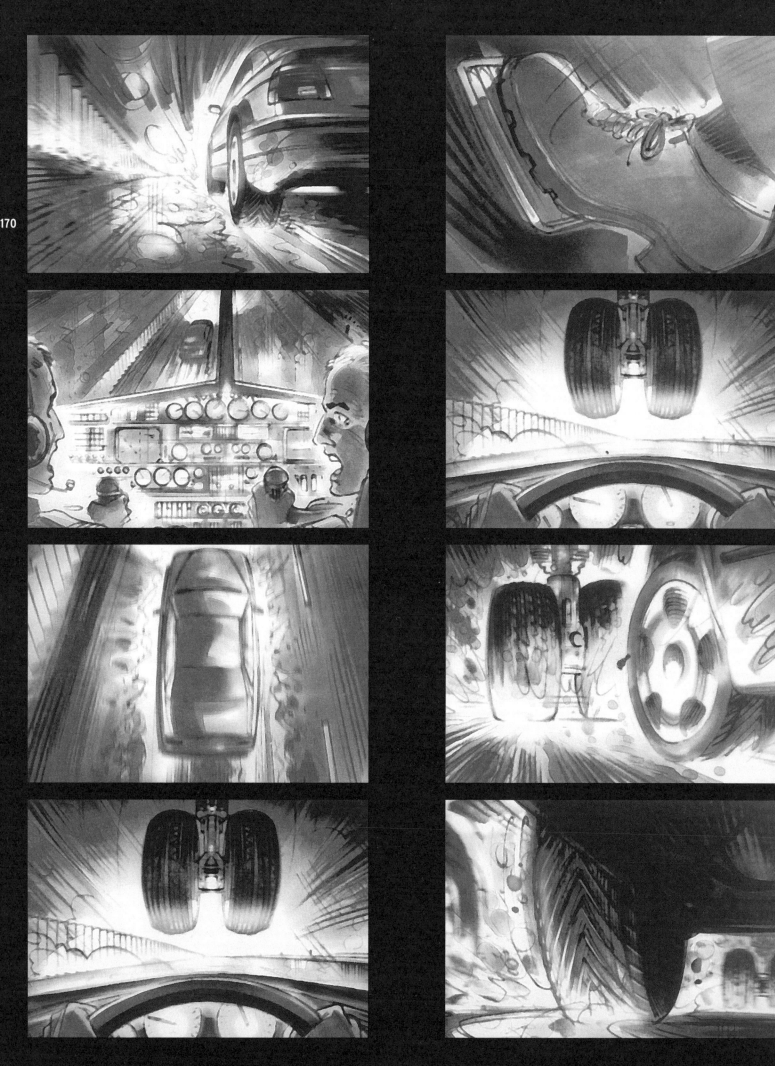

An action-packed storyboard by the agency BBDO for Dunlop tyres. Dramatic viewpoints, strong light/dark contrasts and speedlines show the brand at its best. It's up to you to decide whether your layout looks better on a light or dark background. The closing image focuses on the logo and slogan.

This advert for Lee Jeans by Grey Advertising took shape in three stages. The thumbnail concentrates solely on the basic idea for the image and the wordplay of the headline. The layout shows the colours and the positioning of all the text elements. The finished ad follows the layout and casts a suitably long-legged model for the central role.

„ KOMPLEEZE"

One goal,
three different styles

Stefan Lochmann sketched out this ad campaign for Fun Fries in a few lively lines. Because the gestures and facial expressions of the characters in the story are important to the effect of the ad, he has allowed himself to exaggerate slightly by using cartoon-style figures.

Five layout frames and the corresponding screenshots from an ad for Heinz Curry Sauce. The images, from the agency Michael Conrad and Leo Burnett, use a quiet, still and fuss-free treatment to dramatize the old man's moment of pleasure. The 15-second ad was shot on location in Copenhagen.

Here are two very different
storyboards by the illustrator
Hansi Helle. Below, his
characters bring to life an
action-packed ad for the
Wundermann agency, using
crisp colours, radical changes
of perspective and speedlines
that fly out of the frame, giving
a real feeling of movement.

Opposite, stark black and white
gives a very different feel to
this ad for Prinzen cookies
from the firm De Beukelaer,
featuring a prince as its central
character. The strong contrasts
and striking graphic quality
have their own appeal and
show how important it is to
find the right combination of
light and shade for layouts.
Speedlines also play a part.

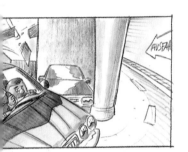

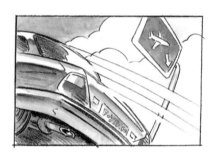

BOOK TIP
*How to Draw Comics
the Marvel Way,*
Stan Lee and John Buscema,
New York: Simon and
Schuster, 1978

Is it love? It's more than that –
it's a great concept for a Mini
campaign by the Hamburg ad
agency Jung von Matt. The
panoramic images of the
storyboard use fairly simple
lines to convey the winding
journey of the two friends in
the speedy little car. Speedlines
emphasize the exaggerated
perspective and make the
action clearer.

Opposite, two concepts for
Mini billboards shown in
chronological order, beginning
with the thumbnails. In the
centre, the comprehensive
layouts combine marker images
with digital typography. Below
are the finished ads, enough
to make any motorist's heart
beat a little faster.

176

[B O O K   T I P
Presentation Techniques:
A Guide to Drawing and
Presenting Design Ideas,
Dick Powell, London:
Macdonald, 1990]

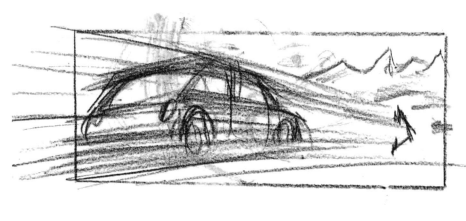

IS IT LOVE ?

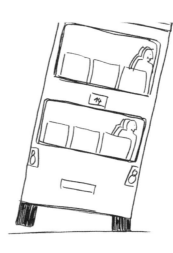

IS IT LOVE ?

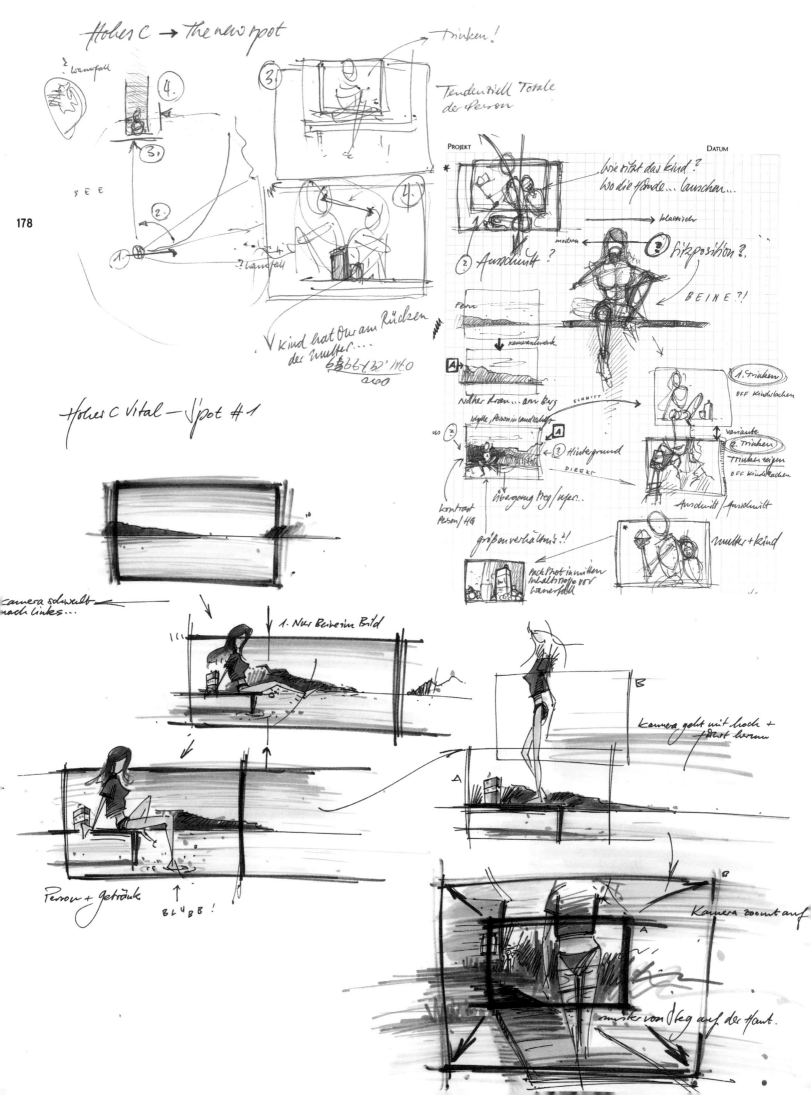

These thumbnails and layouts for 'Höhe C' fruit drink illustrate the working methods of the Frankfurt-based team Vier-für-Texas. They clearly show the search for the best possible approach and the discussion on how to bring together the themes of family and good health in a convincing way.

Trying things out, discussing them with colleagues and improving them is the best way to come up with a great finished ad. The comprehensive storyboard below looks really effective, with its roughly drawn frames accentuating the sketchlike feel of the artwork.

⑥ In Annas Gesicht sieht man, dass sie das kühle Getränk genießt. Es ist genauso natürlich wie ihre Umgebung.

[Das Kinderlachen wiederholt sich...]

① Wir erleben einen sonnigen Frühlingsmorgen an einem ruhigen, abgelegenen See. Der Wald spiegelt sich auf der glatten Oberfläche. Im Hintergrund kann man einen Wasserfall entdecken, der frisches Quellwasser in den See bringt.

⑦

② Nichts Schöneres, als hier die nackten Füße ins kühle Wasser zu strecken. Anna hat Lust dazu. Genüsslich taucht sie ihren Fuß in das Wasser des Sees.

⑧ Sie setzt das Glas zum zweiten mal an und trinkt erneut.

[Noch einmal wiederholt sich das Kinderlachen im Moment des Trinkens ...]

③

Sie freut sich auf ein Glas hohes C Vital – greift nach der Packung, schenkt sich ein ...

④ OFF:
»Jetzt gibt es das neue hohes C Vital – aus besten Früchten und sanften Pflanzen-extrakten von Malve, Ginkgo und Artischocke. Das erfrischt und stärkt sie von Innen. «

⑨ Anna dreht sich zu ihrer Tochter, die sich sanft an ihren Rücken kuschelt...

[Ein angenehmes Schluckgeräusch ist zu hören. Die Tochter horcht neugierig am Rücken ihrer Mutter, wie das Getränk beim Schlucken im Körper gluckert. Beide müssen lachen...]

⑤ ...und trinkt.
In diesem Moment ist sie ganz bei sich und der Natur.

[Während des Trinkens ist ein helles Kinderlachen zu hören. Es fängt leise an und steigert sich vergnügt...]

⑩ Packshot hohes C Vital umgeben von einem Arrangement aus Früchten und Kräutern.

OFF:
»hohes C Vital – in den Geschmacksrichtungen Apfel-Pfirsich-Maracuja und Traube-Kirsche. Mit sanften Pflanzenextrakten und wertvollen B-Vitaminen.

hohes C Vital. Einfach wohlfühlen von Innen. «

What's the best way to demonstrate an new automatic car with an amazingly smooth multitronic transmission to replace the jerky transmissions of earlier automatics? Frankfurt-based Saatchi & Saatchi creatives Harald Wittig and Benjamin Lommel gave a memorable answer to that question with their ad 'The Fan'.

The ad is funny, the casting spot-on, and the wobbling Elvis doll ended up becoming a craze in Germany. The ad was made by Jo!Schmid Productions and filmed on location in South Africa. The traditionally styled storyboard below is by the illustrator Frank Schlief (www.kritzeltiere.de).

180

Video:
An Elvis fan drives along the road, listening to an Elvis song.

He changes gear in time with the music.

The jerky gear change makes the Elvis doll on his dashboard start wobbling in time to the music.

He watches the doll dancing and smiles to himself.

Then his car engine gives up the ghost.

Audio:
Song: 'King of the Road'
SFX: Engine noise

Song
SFX: Gear change

Song

Song

Song
SFX: The engine splutters and then dies.

Video:
He asks if he can put some music on and the driver doesn't mind.

The fan puts his Elvis doll on the same place on the dashboard.

But the doll doesn't move, even when the A4 changes gear. The fan stares at the doll and then at the driver.

Then he looks at the doll again.

It's still not moving.

Audio:
SFX: The A4 slowly accelerates.

The song begins again.

Song

Song

Song

SAATCHI & SAATCHI

...packs up his belongings ...d waits for a lift.

An Audi A4 approaches.

The Audi A4 stops. The Elvis fan leans over by the passenger window, smiles and gets in.

...X: A car approaches

...inally he pushes the doll ...ith his finger, and it starts ...ancing again.

Caption:
Multitronic. The first super-smooth automatic transmission.

The A4 drives away.

multitronic.
Die erste
wirklich stufen-
lose Automatik.

...Song

SFX: The Audi A4 accelerates.

SFX: The Audi A4 accelerates.

This TV ad for the Schwäbische Hall building society was created by Ogilvy & Mather. The [shooting board] is arranged in a clear, simple row. It was developed by the agency from a treatment, in collaboration with the director. Looking at the storyboard frames, you can see the striking camera angles and the lively cuts between the actors.

This underlines the dialogue of the ad, and allows us to empathize with the young characters. The director puts the focus on the idea of teenagers talking, using a realistic [POV] and placing the viewer right in the middle of the action.

Bausparkasse Schwäbisch Hall
TV-Spot "Teenies" 30 Sekunden

Shootingboard

"... my parents will be away for 3 weeks y'know..."

"Really...?"
"Yeah...we'll have the whole house for ourselves..."

"Cool!"

"Look they have a pool here..."

"Yeah.... You like that?"

"3 weeks of party...!"

"Meine Eltern...
"...fahren 3 Wochen weg."

"Echt...?"
"Wir haben das ganze Haus für uns..."

"Cool!"

"Schau mal, die haben 'nen Pool..."

"ja, ...magst Du das?"
3 Wochen Party."

"Ey, wir feiern draußen."

"Klare Ansage:
3 Wochen Party"

Arrows and speedlines are used to move the viewer's gaze from one image to the next. The dialogue below the frames is written in two languages: German for the final ad, and English so that the Swedish director of the ad could follow it.

Bausparkasse Schwäbisch Hall
TV-Spot „Teenies"
30 Sekunden

Wir sind in einem typischen Jugendzimmer. Zwei Mädels schauen sich Fotos an, während Tommy auf dem Sofa liegt und verträumt ins Blaue schaut.
Plötzlich sagt Tommy:

Tommy:	Meine Eltern fahren 3 Wochen weg.
Steffi:	Echt?
Tommy:	Wir haben das ganze Haus für uns.
Steffi:	Ey, cool.
Tommy:	(Ohne Text)
Elke:	Schau mal, die haben nen Pool.
Steffi:	Ey, wir feiern draussen.
Tommy:	Klare Ansage: Drei Wochen Party.
Elke:	Sag mal, sind Deine Eltern eigentlich Millionäre?
Tommy:	Nööö. ... Die sind ... eigentlich ... eher Bausparer ...
Off:	Vier Wände und alles was Sie für die Zukunft brauchen. Schwäbisch Hall. Auf diese Steine können Sie bauen.

Fuchs und Logo erscheinen, der Jingle ertönt.

The concept was presented to the client in the form of the lively hand-drawn storyboard below, drawn by Stockholm-based illustrator Johan Unenge.

"Say... are your parents millionaires?"

"Naah... they are... you know....to be honest ....saving into a building society.."

VoiceOver:
"Four Walls and everything you need for your Future."

VoiceOver:
"Schwäbisch Hall ... (to be cont.)"

"Sag mal, sind Deine Eltern eigentlich Millionäre?"

"Nööö, ... die sind ... eigentlich ... eher ... Bausparer......"

"Vier Wände und...."

"....alles was Sie für die Zukunft brauchen. Schwäbisch Hall. Auf diese Steine können Sie bauen."

The Hamburg agency Springer
& Jacoby present and sell their
film ideas primarily in the form
of [**treatments**]. The next
phase involves the production
of hand-drawn [**shooting
boards**]. These are discussed
with the client at a [**PPM**]
before the ad is made. These
two ads for Belmondo shoes
(opposite) and Fisherman's
Friend (below) speak for
themselves and for the value
of good ideas.

Treatment for a TV ad for
Fisherman's Friend.

Ultraromantic scene. We see
a couple kissing passionately.
And they keep on kissing and
kissing. Suddenly, the man
breaks away from the woman
and gasps for breath. The
camera cuts to the woman.
With a smile on her lips, she
reveals a Fisherman's Friend
clenched between her teeth.
A huge wave thunders out at
the TV screen.

Pack shot. VO and caption:
'Fisherman's Friend. If they're
too strong, you're too weak.'

B O O K   T I P

*The Empire Strikes
Back Notebook*,
Diana Attias and
Lindsay Smith, New York:
Ballantine Books, 1980

The [**shooting board**] for
the ad was done in pencil
in a highly expressive style.

Treatment for 20-second 'UFO' ad for Belmondo shoes.

We see the endless reaches of outer space. An impressive spaceship looms over our planet. Cut to the UFO control room: terrifying creatures from outer space babble in a language we can't understand.

Here are the subtitles:
'Commander, an inhabited planet!'
'Destroy!'
'Destroy?!'
'Yes. Warp 9.5. Prepare photon torpedoes. Set phasers to full power.'

The evil aliens cackle with laughter. They prepare to land, in the middle of the pavement. At that exact moment the mini UFO gets totally flattened... by a Belmondo shoe.
Voiceover: 'Belmondo. Exclusively from Görtz.'

The 'UFO' shooting board gets the idea across with relatively little artistic effort.

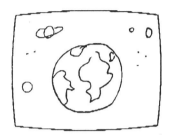

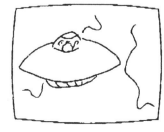

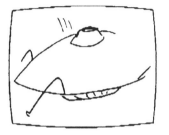

In the storyboard opposite, 'Kebab Connection', for the Hamburg production company Wüste Film, Dawn Parisi plunges right into the action. Exaggerated perspectives and action-packed scenes bring the planned plot to life in Cinemascope format (1: 2.33). The sketchy pencil lines look dynamic but are also well suited to correction-heavy designs. Nonetheless, this project required five days and around 110 individual images to get down on paper. Sources used included architectural plans of the locations, photos of the actors, set and costume designs, and detailed descriptions from the director and cameraman.

The Hamburg-based illustrator Dawn Parisi (www.dawnparisi.com) produced this storyboard for Markenfilm Hamburg in a graphic comic-book style. Despite the two-dimensionality of the harsh black and white, she uses changing viewpoints and framing to give a filmic look to the story. The board, presented in a traditional format, looks exciting and gives a sense of movement. Arrows that show motion are a key part of Dawn's work.

[B O O K   T I P

Cinematography,
Peter Ettedgui,
Woburn, MA: Focal
Press, 1998]

SL Stefan Lochmann • Art Direction • Film • Adelheidstraße 56 • 65185 Wiesbaden   Tel: 0611   30 81 630 • Fax: 0611   30 81

E	Motiv	Einstellung	Cast
1	STUDIO	TOTAL DÄMON IM STUDIO DURCHDREHEN BIS SESSELDREHUNG	DÄMON
2	STUDIO	FAHRT AUF CU DAMON	DÄMON
3 7	STUDIO	CU MUND DÄMON	DÄMON
4	STUDIO	CU HAND AM SCHIEBEREGLER	DÄMON
6	STUDIO	CU KATZENAUGE	DÄMON
5	STUDIO	HAND NIMMT VIDEOTAPE + SCHIEBT ES IN DEN RECORDER	DÄMON

	Text	Time Code	Video
kung			
TIVE MIT POLCAT LTON ZUM ABHÄNGEN 3×5 m EORECORDER NITOR	THIS IS THE BEGINNING	0:00	
UNTER LICHT	THIS IS THE BEGINNING	0:00	
UNTERLICHT	THIS IS THE BEGINNING —— PROG. ATTACK	0:01	
RAMATISCHES STREIFLICHT		0:04	
		0:08	
SSETTE ROT O GRAU I LABEL (SL)		0 06	

Kunde: Edel Titel: The Theme/Progressive Attack Regie. Stefan Lochmann Datum: 03.12.96

Produktion: Der Filmtempel, A. Rumpf Länge: 3:57 Künstler: Brooklyn Bounce Kamera: Eckhard Jansen Seite: 1

B O O K   T I P
From Star Wars to Indiana Jones:
The Best of the Lucasfilm Archives,
Mark Cotta Voz and Shinji Hata,
San Francisco: Chronicle, 1994

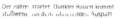

Der Fahrer startet. Dunkler Rauch kommt stoßweise aus dem röhrenden Auspuff

Das Auto verläßt die Tankstelle, an der keine Person zu sehen ist. Auch die Straßen sind menschenleer.

Aus der Ferne rast das Auto heran. Kamera in Bodennähe.

Blick aus dem Dunkeln auf die beleuchtete Stadt.

Aufnahme aus dem Inneren des Autos. Ein Schild mit der Aufschrift: "You are leaving New York State" Fahrer: "Alles in Ordnung"

Why should a storyboard have to look like

Der Tankwart reibt mit einem Schwamm die zerquetschten Insektenleichen vom Kühlergrill und den Scheinwerfern. Haben sie's noch weit?

Kamera zoomt aufs Ohr des Fahrers. Man hört von draußen die gedämpfte Stimme des Tankwarts rufen. Hey!

Geräusche gehen über in Stimmengewirr. Musik und Partygeräusche sind hörbar.

Eine Frau in rotem Kleid fragt: "Wo gehst du denn hin Schatz?"

Der Mann verläßt das Zimmer. Man sieht den Volvo in der offenen Garage. Er sagt: "Nicht weit! Nur an die frische Luft!"

Der Fahrer steigt ins Auto und schließt die Tür

Schnitt beim Knallen der Autotür. Das Auto gibt Vollgas und rast mit quietschenden Reifen aus der Tankstelle. Tankwart: "Hey, was soll das denn? Ich hab doch nur gefragt!!"

Der Fahrer biegt wieder auf dem Highway

Er tatscheit das Armaturenbrett und sagt:
Nicht mehr lange, und wir sind in Buffalo.

Mittlerweile fahrt das Auto auf der Pennsylvania Interstate
Im Hintergrund liegt still und grau der Eriesee

Fahrer zu seinem Volvo:
"Laß dich von Cleveland nicht runterziehen."

Von einer Tankstelle aus sieht man den Volvo
langsam auf die Zapfsäulen zurollen

a storyboard?

This question was put to Wiesbaden students, who then tried to find alternative ways of presenting layouts for films and ads.

The result was a series of [moodboards], comic-book panels and experimental collages which attempt to translate film techniques – cuts, tracking shots, motion – into visual compositions. The legibility and drama of comic strips provided inspiration and were used to make the plot of

the film clear. This example by Thomas Heger is a storyboard of a short story by John Irving. The changing shots add movement, supported by the alternating wide and narrow formats, the arrangement of shots into strips and the overlapping of the start and end with zoom shots.

Kamera sinkt aus Vogelstand-
punkt langsam tiefer

Chicago, Großstadtlärm

David Bascom brings extra life to his images by arranging them in an unconventional way. By alternating between extremely wide shots and tall, narrow details, and cutting up some of the story, he adds excitement and movement. The contrast of broad and thin, light and dark, near and far are skilfully rendered to add drama to the whole piece. David's work is another example of the use of comic-strip panels to grab the viewer's attention.

The End...

B O O K   T I P S

Rendering With Markers, Ronald B. Kemnitzer, New York: Watson-Guptill, 1983

Moebius Zeichenwelt, ed. Andreas Platthaus, Frankfurt: Eichborn, 2003

The Illustrated Star Wars Universe, Ralph McQuarrie and Kevin J. Anderson, London: Bantam, 1995

Made it! After lap after lap of layouts, we're on the home stretch. We hope that all our suggestions and tips, plus a few glances over the shoulders of the professionals, will help you visualize your ideas quickly and professionally in future. Use our ideas in any way you like and, most of all, develop your own personal style. And of course if you want to improve you've got to practise. However, remember one thing: never lose the element of fun. You'll see that anything can work if you want it to. And now: go out and get to work!

Speedlines can clarify, signal the unexpected, emphasize emotions or bring flat surfaces to life. It's up to you to decide what role you want them to play.

Susanne Schwalm also tries to find a balance between conventional storyboard presentation and giving a sense of visual animation. Her interpretation of the theme of an invisible fly trying to get out of a room is given a new dimension through this collage-style presentation.

These few examples show that the visualization of ideas for films is a great place for experimentation.

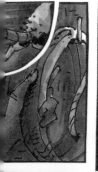

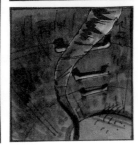

A ready-to-use storyboard template

So that you can concentrate on the ideas and the design for your film, without having to worry about the dull practicalities of presentation, here is a standard storyboard template. It can be enlarged, reduced, rearranged and changed in any way that you like, to suit the project you're working on.

Picture formats are named according to the ratio between the length and width of the screen. Some of the most commonly found formats are shown below:

The left-hand side is for notes and comments on the story and technical details such as [POV], camera angles, lighting and special effects.

The right-hand side is for dialogue and sound effects.

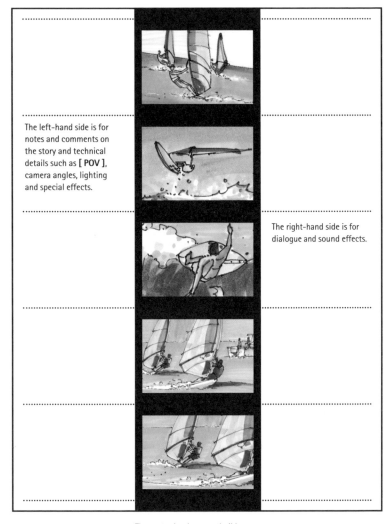

The centre is where you build up the sequence of images for the story. The black ground means that it doesn't matter if the lines go outside of the boxes: they won't be visible.

To personalize your storyboard, you should mark the top of your page with your signature or logo. The top of the page is also where you should list the project name, client and film length. If need be, you can cut the template down and stick it to a larger sheet to create more space for corporate information.

1: 1.33 format
US standard, TV and computer monitors

1: 1.66 format
European standard and 16mm film

1: 1.85 cinema format
US standard projection

1: 2.35 superwide format
Cinerama and Cinescope

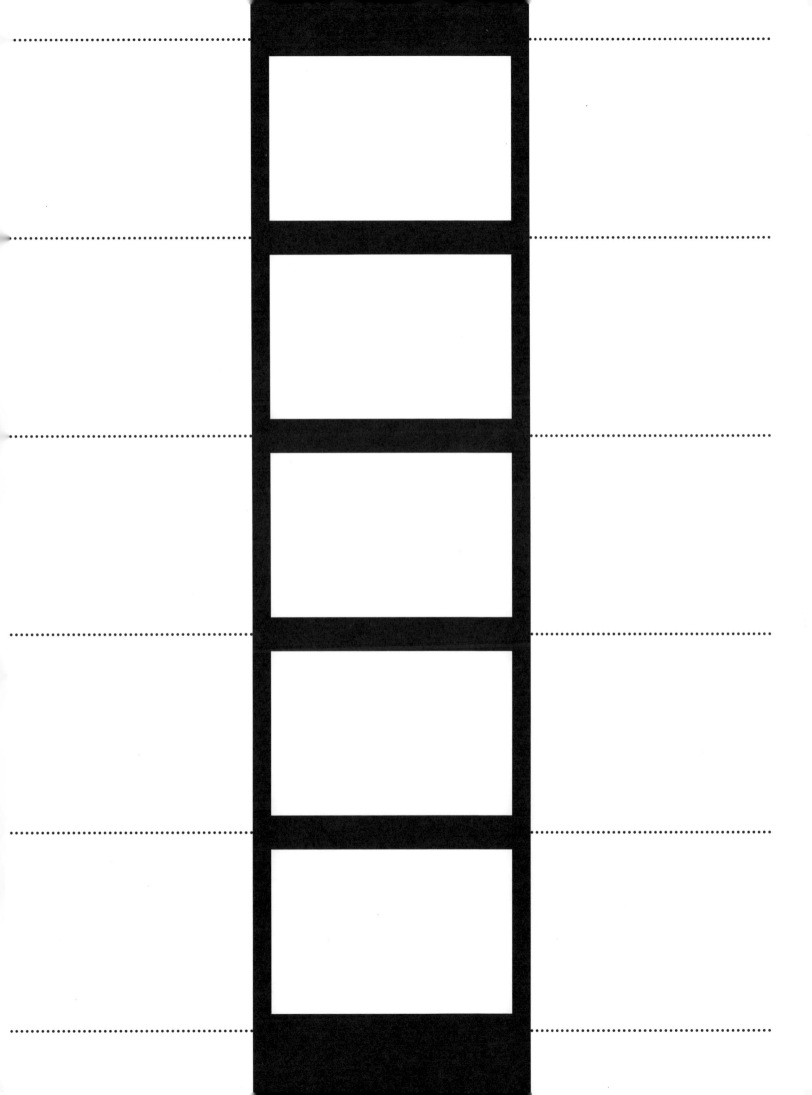

Common mistakes and how to avoid them

Here and overleaf, we've brought together a set of examples of the things that most commonly go wrong with layouts. Because criticism alone is never very helpful, we've also pointed out how

they could be improved. Look at the results of our before-and-after comparisons and check out the earlier chapters of this book for more examples. Better still, why not try to improve these drawings

yourself? With a bit of luck, you should be able to avoid making similar mistakes in future. (Note: all the examples on these pages are reproduced at around 50 per cent of their original size.)

Pages 32–37

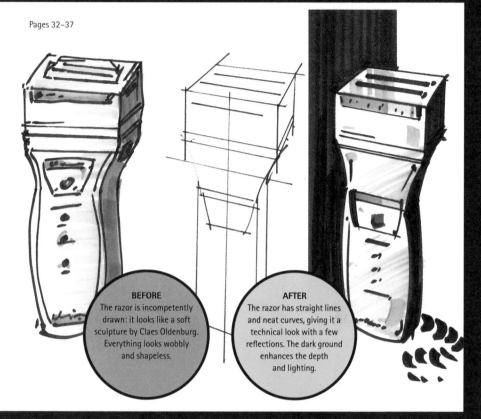

BEFORE
The razor is incompetently drawn: it looks like a soft sculpture by Claes Oldenburg. Everything looks wobbly and shapeless.

AFTER
The razor has straight lines and neat curves, giving it a technical look with a few reflections. The dark ground enhances the depth and lighting.

Pages 18–19 and 24–25

BEFORE
Messy outlines and criss-crossing corrected strokes. Ellipses are wobbly and the perspective is wrong, with the table top shown in profile but the objects shown from above.

AFTER
Quickly drawn strokes create a lively drawing with a combination of freehand and ruled lines. The perspective has been corrected.

Pages 28–31

BEFORE
Bad rendering of materials: the glass sphere is deformed and bumpy due to overcorrection, while the fabric lacks elegance and lightness because its lines are much too heavy.

AFTER
The sphere has a smooth outline, created by drawing around the bottom of a can. The folds in the fabric are drawn with fast upward strokes, and pale colours have been lightly applied.

Pages 62–65 and 70–71

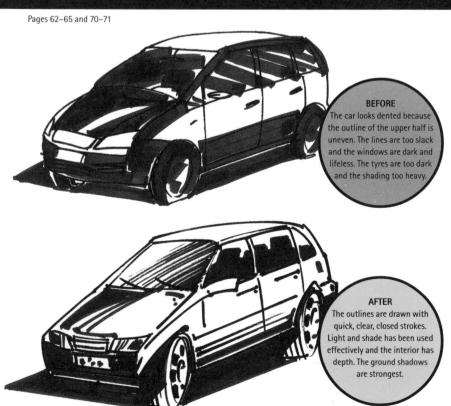

BEFORE
The car looks dented because the outline of the upper half is uneven. The lines are too slack and the windows are dark and lifeless. The tyres are too dark and the shading too heavy.

AFTER
The outlines are drawn with quick, clear, closed strokes. Light and shade has been used effectively and the interior has depth. The ground shadows are strongest.

Pages 64–71

Pages 38–47

Pages 83–87

Pages 42–45 and 96–9797

Pages 78–81

BEFORE
The heavy black lines make the sand into strict geometric shapes, contradicting its true grainy structure. The monochrome colour palette has too little contrast.

AFTER
The lines are fast and light, making everything look more free and unstructured. The lighting is more subtle but still monochrome; the sky is calmer and paler.

BEFORE
Dark and chaotic reflection lines dominate this still life. Light had shade are carelessly applied to the surfaces. The background is messy, the colours patchy.

Pages 80–83

BEFORE
The foreground detail is too undeveloped; it turns into a mix of lines, colours and patterns. The colours look dirty and the background is too heavy.

AFTER
The colours are brighter and the contrasts greater. The foreground is lighter and more linear; the background detail is just hinted at. Everything looks more spacious.

AFTER
The light source is clear, so the coloured areas are more effective. Colour contrasts have been increased; pale blue instead of grey is used for the foam. The background is neat.

Pages 76–83

BEFORE
It's impossible to tell what the details are meant to be; the shapes, lines and colours merge into one another and make the picture look messy. All the detail has been lost.

AFTER
The landscape is structured and has a sense of light. The number of lines has been reduced; the coloured areas are carefully placed. It's easy to tell buildings and trees apart.

Pages 44–49

BEFORE
The hand has too many details and the lines are too heavy. The fingers seem to dominate. All the lines seem slightly wobbly as if the image has been badly traced.

AFTER
The lines vary in thickness and are done in quick bold strokes. The outlines are partially open, and the fingers have been treated as a mass. The hand looks more elegant.

Pages 126–127

BEFORE
Faces are too flat, lifeless and too heavily coloured. Chin lines too heavy, hair lumpy and uneven. Above, neck too curved; below, nostril in wrong place. Eyes look dead and dark, or invisible.

199

Pages 110–115 and 144–149

BEFORE
Wobbly lines, drawn too slowly. Outlines too heavy and flat. Details like the mouth and hand are badly drawn. Neck too curved, waist too thick, and folds of fabric ignored. Looks unfeminine.

AFTER
Looks much more feminine; lines are bold and quick with the fabric folds drawn correctly. Tracing has added more solidity. Hair and neck are correct and mouth and sunglasses are hinted at.

AFTER
Quick, curving strokes make both images lighter and more lively. Shading adds depth, eyes dominate, other features are simplified or omitted. Necks are straight and slim.

Pages 80–83 and 95

AFTER
The tree trunk looks organic and the leaves are simplified. The base of the tree is anchored to the landscape and the ground is suggested with naturally flowing lines.

BEFORE
The tree and landscape both look like a child's drawing: simple, heavily outlined and flat. The tree isn't anchored to the landscape. It will be hard to add colour later.

[Account] The relationship between an ad agency and a client, which may last for one campaign or may be ongoing.

[Acetate] A transparent sheet of plastic, often used for overlays in layouts.

[Advertorial] A paid-for print ad that resembles a news article or editorial; usually identified by the word 'Advertisement' printed along the top of the page.

[Airbrush] A technique that uses a compressed air spray and ink to create smooth colour gradations. See COPIC Airbrush System.

[Animatic] An elaborate means of presenting an idea for a film. There are two ways of doing this:
• Static pictures are filmed and then edited together with sound and visual effects to create the illusion of movement.
• A large-format layout is produced that enables tracking shots, panning and other techniques to be used during filming. The feeling of movement can also be increased through the cartoon-like technique of adding or removing extra picture elements while the main image remains static.
If photographic images rather than illustrations are used, the result is sometimes known as a videomatic.

[Art buyer] An agency professional whose task is to organize and buy in creative services from outside the agency, such as freelance photographers, illustrators and layout artists.

[Art director] The agency creative in charge of the visual aspects of an idea. He or she works with a copywriter to develop, visualize and present these ideas to clients and work towards the finished ad.

[Benefit] Any feature of a product that is highlighted in an ad. The most important benefits are that the product is better or cheaper than its competitors.

[Bleed] Allowing an image or ad to extend over the margins of a printed page.

[Bleedproof paper] Coated layout paper that doesn't allow ink to seep through.

[Bleed-through technique] The deliberate use of markers on uncoated paper, so that the marker ink seeps through the top sheet onto the paper underneath, to create subtle colour effects.

[Blue screen] A technique in which objects or people are filmed against a blue background, which is then easy to remove and replace in post-production. Green screen is also used.

[Brief] An outline of the aims and rules of an ad campaign; this is agreed between the agency and the client before work begins.

[Casting] The search for suitable models and actors for photos and films.

[Comprehensive layout or Comp] A layout of an ad designed to be presented to the client, sufficiently detailed as to appear very close to how the finished ad will look.

[COPIC Layout System]
• **[COPIC Marker]**: this versatile alcohol-based marker is dual-ended, with one thin tip for sketching and one broad nib for filling in larger areas. Refillable with replaceable nibs.
• **[COPIC Wide]**: with its 21mm-wide nib, this pen is ideal for filling of large areas of colour and backgrounds. Refillable with replaceable nibs.
• **[COPIC Multiliner SP]**: an inking pen available in nine different widths, refillable and with replaceable nibs. Its fine lines will not smudge even when coloured in with markers.
• **[COPIC Sketch]**: a brush-like pen that produces very soft outlines.
• **[COPIC Various Inks]**: a range of inks that can be used to refill COPIC pens and can also be mixed to create new colours.
• **[COPIC Colorless Blender]**: a special solvent that can be applied to COPIC inks with a refillable pen, to create graduated tones.
• **[COPIC Airbrush System]**: COPIC markers can be inserted into an adapter and used with an air compressor to create airbrush effects and fill large surface areas.
• **[COPIC Opaque White]**: an opaque ink that can be applied with a brush to produce white highlights.
• **[COPIC Marker Pads]**: bleedproof layout paper, available in various formats.
• **[COPIC Ink Absorber]**: a holder with disposable pads that can be used to smear wet ink and cover large areas, or used in conjunction with Colorless Blender to create smoothly graduated shading.

[Copy] The written text or spoken words for an ad.

[Copywriter] The person who writes advertising texts (copy) for an agency.

[Creative Director] An agency executive who supervises the creative team and approves projects at all stages.

[Creatives] The art directors and copywriters in an ad agency.

[Crop] To cut off specific portions of an illustration or photograph.

[Cross-fade] A film effect in which the end of one shot is overlapped by the start of the next shot, with the first shot gradually fading away to be replaced by the second one.

[Cutting] An editing technique that creates a quick transition from one filmed scene to another.

[Demographics] A way of describing the audience of an ad according to shared facts about them (such as age, gender, background).

[Dissolve] A gradual fade from one scene to another in a film or TV ad.

[Frame] Term for one illustrated panel in a storyboard. Also a single film or video image (a film has 24 frames per second, a video 25 frames per second).

[Ink absorber] See COPIC Ink Absorber.

[Inlay] Two motifs drawn separately which are then carefully cut out with a scalpel and mounted one on top of or alongside the other. See page 42.

[Layout paper, layout pad] Opaque white paper which has a bleedproof coating on the reverse so that marker ink can't seep through. The layout pad is sturdy and can be turned to any angle you wish, making it an ideal portable drawing table.

[Line pressure] Applying different amounts of pressure to the pen can change the width and density of your lines, and so creates interesting depth effects.

[Mask] These practical aids made of strong, smooth cardboard can be cut out as needed from old layout boards.

[Masking fluid] A solution that can be painted on to areas of a drawing to protect them while background colours or other effects are applied. It dries to a rubbery finish and can be peeled off afterwards.

[Montage technique] When image elements from different sources are brought together and pasted into a single image. See page 112.

Glossary

[Moodboard] A board covered with images cut from magazines and other sources, intended to capture a particular mood or visual theme for an ad or presentation, and to be used as a visual stimulus for designers.

[Opaque white] See COPIC Opaque White.

[Pan] To swing the camera horizontally or vertically, to follow a subject or to give a panoramic effect.

[Paste-up] A camera-ready layout with text and picture material correctly positioned on a backboard, ready for reproduction.

[Pitch] An agency's initial presentation of a campaign strategy to a client.

[Post-production] Work done on an ad once the principal photography or filming is complete.

[POV] Point of view.

[PPM] Pre-production meeting: this takes place before filming of an ad begins, to finalize all necessary details.

[Production board] A complex, structured layout which contains not only the visuals but also more detailed information on shots, location, casting, script and timing (also called a shooting board).

[Psychographics] A way of describing the audience of an ad according to their shared psychological characteristics (such as likes and dislikes).

[Relaunch] Reworking of an existing brand or campaign.

[Rendering] Producing a complete and detailed illustration with features such as light and shade, texture and colour.

[Rendering paper] Brilliant white, slightly transparent paper with a double-sided bleedproof coating, so that both sides can be worked on without marker ink seeping through.

[Retouching] To alter a photograph or piece of artwork to remove imperfections and make changes.

[Rough] An early, unfinished layout for an ad which shows only the basic concepts and content, so that these may be discussed and finalized.

[Rough cut] An early version of a film or ad that is roughly edited together, often without voiceover or music, to give clients or creatives a general idea of what the finished product will be like.

[Scrap file] A collection of images from magazines, newspapers and catalogues which you can use as source material for thumbnails and layouts.

[Semi-comps] Semi-comprehensive layouts, more detailed than roughs but less fully finished than comprehensive layouts.

[Shooting board] See Production board.

[Slogan] Also called a tagline; a phrase of copy that sums up the campaign strategy.

[Speedlines] Lines that indicate movement, used in comics and cartoons.

[Spray adhesive] An aerosol glue that is used for mounting layouts.

[Spread] A pair of facing pages in a publication, or an ad that is printed across two pages.

[Steadicam] A special camera which is attached to the body of the camera operator, so that he or she can move freely during filming but the image will remain steady throughout.

[Storyboard] The plot of a film or ad, broken down into a series of individual pictures, and captioned with notes on dialogue, sound effects and filming. See page 150.

[Storyboard template] A ready-made frame that you can used to draw your own storyboards easily. Pre-printed storyboard pads are also available, with a central row of frames and space on both sides for notes and directions.

[Target group] A specific audience for which an advertising campaign is designed.

[Templates] For comprehensive layouts, where presentation and neatness are important, these can be a useful tool for drawing circles or ellipses.

[Thumbnail] A small rough sketch used to show a basic layout or picture idea.

[Tracking shot] A type of film shot in which the camera follows a moving subject at a constant distance, so that the subject remains sharply focused while the background looks blurred.

[Transparency] A photograph or illustration on clear acetate film, which may be overlaid on top of a background image.

[Treatment] A brief description of a film or ad.

[TVC] Television commercial.

[USP] Unique Selling Point - a benefit of a product that makes it different from rival brands, and is therefore emphasized in advertising.

[VO] Voiceover.

And to finish, a big thank you...

Any layout, no matter what the
theme, needs the right team to
make it happen. Our thanks to
everyone whose layouts appear
in this book, and to Thommy
Mallmann for the lively image
shown above

ur thanks to all of those who helped to create this ook. Without them, it would have been a much ore difficult task. First and foremost, our thanks all our students at Wiesbaden. When their work ppears in this book, it is printed with the student's ame alongside it. Unfortunately, it wasn't always ossible to clearly assign every piece of work to a udent, so our apologies for this! We thought it was mportant to include any piece of work that was uitable for demonstration purposes and that llustrated the level of professionalism of the Wiesbaden course. Uncredited images are by he authors themselves.

Thanks to all the agencies, firms and professionals who allowed us to reproduce their work:

BBDO Werbeagentur, Düsseldorf
Björn Koop, Estland
Grey Advertising, Düsseldorf
Norbert Guthier, Frankfurt
Hansi Helle, Sulzbach
Heller & Partner, Berlin
Jung von Matt, Hamburg
Frauke Kärcher, Munich
Thommy Mallmann, Berlin
Lesch + Frey Werbeagentur, Frankfurt
Stefan Lochmann, Wiesbaden
Michael Conrad & Leo Burnett, Frankfurt
Dawn Parisi, Hamburg
Ogilvy & Mather, Frankfurt
Ruske & Pühretmaier, Wiesbaden
Saatchi & Saatchi Advertising, Frankfurt
Frank Schlief, Hamburg
Susanne Schwalm, Wiesbaden
Bernhard Speh, Wiesbaden
Springer & Jacoby, Hamburg
TBWA\ Werbeagentur
Johan Unenge, Stockholm
Vier-für-Texas, Frankfurt
Wundermann, Frankfurt
Young & Rubicam, Frankfurt

Thanks to the students of the University for Applied Sciences in Wiesbaden, who included:

Ute Bach
David Bascom
Marisa Boonyaprasop
Joachim Brandenberg
Julia Maria Depis
Christian Felder
Dirk Frömmer
Anja Ganster
Jens Hartmann
Thomas Heger
Jörn C. Hofmann
Peter Kohl
Jonas Kramer
Marloes Kremers
Heike Kreutzmann
Tim Leydecker
Christina Männel
Sven Müller
Uwe Neitzel
Veronique Noçon
Dennis Nußbaum
Guido Pechaczek
Jörg Pelka
Sina Preikschat
Silvia Püchner
Markus Remscheid
Mathias Schäfer
Jürgen Schanz
Susanne Schwalm
Rüdiger Schwarzkopf
Jasmin Siddiqui
Stefan Sperner
Daniel Springer
Florian Stucki
Daniela Völlger
Michael Weihnert
Steffen Winkler
Silvia Wolff
Alexandra Zöller

And thanks to all those who worked with us:

Karin and Bertram Schmidt-Friderichs from Verlag Hermann Schmidt Mainz for their constructive conversations and inspiring ideas.

Peter Holtz-Kathan for his encouragement, patience and support for this project throughout its development.

Marian Nestmann and his Mac, who worked on the design and layout for as long as it took to make everything perfect.

Rui Camilo for the photos and the coffee.

Helen and Robin, our ballroom-dancing models. Cha-cha-cha!

And especially to all our loved ones, who are happy that this book is finally finished.

Translated from the German *Ideen visualisieren*

First published in the United Kingdom in 2006 by
Thames & Hudson Ltd, 181A High Holborn, London WC1V 7QX

www.thamesandhudson.com

Original edition © 2004 Verlag Hermann Schmidt, Mainz
This edition © 2006 Thames & Hudson Ltd, London

British Library Cataloguing-in-Publication Data
A catalogue record for this book is available from the British Library

ISBN-13: 978-0-500-28612-8
ISBN-10: 0-500-28612-4

Printed in China